# 60 Model Essays

LIKE TEST PREP

Copyright © 2012 LIKE TEST PREP

All rights reserved.

**ISBN-10: 1479181919**
**ISBN-13: 978-1479181919**

------------------------------------------

Disclaimer: The opinions expressed herein are those of the author and not of the publisher, LIKE TEST PREP.

# CONTENTS

Write a Test Essay in 25 Min.     1

How to Write a Test Essay     3

1   Are actions more important to consider than people's intentions?     11

2   Which is better for society: when its members simply follow the ideas of their leaders or when its members act as individuals?     15

3   Are mainstream views and ideas more likely to be valid?     20

4   Is it better for people to be realistic than optimistic?     25

5   Should government employ everything at their disposal to protect its citizens?     28

6   Are some dreams worth the ultimate price—death?     32

7   Should education emphasize creativity as much as literacy and mathematics?     35

8   Is happiness the result of one's decision to be content in life?     39

9   Which is more important to the international community: the nation-state or the individual?     43

| | | |
|---|---|---|
| 10 | Is apathy just as harmful to humans as causing physical pain? | 48 |
| 11 | Is striving to achieve a goal always the best course of action, or should people give up if they are not making progress? | 52 |
| 12 | Are people more efficient when confronted with the expectations and demands of others? | 56 |
| 13 | Should people quit pursuing their goals when all hope is lost? | 60 |
| 14 | Where do values and belief held by society come from? | 64 |
| 15 | Are conquered dreams and aspirations of people the definition of success? | 68 |
| 16 | Does the media provide an accurate analysis of the events today? | 71 |
| 17 | Is it better to rush sometimes and take action, or is it better to take time and investigate first? | 74 |
| 18 | Should humor be the preferred route for approaching difficult situations and problems? | 78 |
| 19 | Are all people dependent on a social network and family, even if they choose a life of solitude? | 82 |
| 20 | Do you agree that our society has | 85 |

become too negative and less sensitive?

| 21 | Do you believe art and creativity should always be associated with anguish, suffering, and pain? | 89 |
| 22 | Is life predetermined or do people have the ability to pave their own paths in life? | 93 |
| 23 | Should the definition of courage be restricted to people who risk their own well-being for the good of others or should it also be expanded to people who uphold values? | 96 |
| 24 | Is it feasible for a society to simultaneously offer perfect equality and perfect freedom? | 99 |
| 25 | Are there social situations when impolite behavior is necessary? | 102 |
| 26 | Does ethical behavior impede the pursuit of success? | 105 |
| 27 | What is more reflective of personal character: actions or words? | 109 |
| 28 | Are lives improved when changes are made? | 112 |
| 29 | What important qualities are shared by famous or successful people? | 115 |
| 30 | What plays a larger role for achieving success: effort or good fortune? | 118 |

| | | |
|---|---|---|
| 31 | Do television images of immoral behavior and violence make society immoral and dangerous? | 122 |
| 32 | Is war sometimes necessary? | 126 |
| 33 | Has today's abundance of information only made it more difficult for us to understand the world around us? | 130 |
| 34 | Is courage a human trait that is dormant with little opportunity to be used or demonstrated? | 134 |
| 35 | Should people plan for good things to happen to them, or should they depend on the idea of destiny to bring good fortune? | 137 |
| 36 | Do you believe the love of money is the root of all evil? | 140 |
| 37 | Are memories of past events central to understanding ourselves? | 143 |
| 38 | Does the road to success or to failure involve pleasing people? | 146 |
| 39 | Do you believe the criteria for justice is set and molded only by the strong and victorious? | 149 |
| 40 | Do we detest the flaws in others that we see in ourselves? | 152 |
| 41 | Should society censure some kinds of | 155 |

information or forms of expression?

| | | |
|---|---|---|
| 42 | Is it always advantageous to pool the efforts and traits of people to reach the most effective solution for any given problem? | 158 |
| 43 | Does comparison with others allow people to appreciate what they have as individuals? | 162 |
| 44 | Should long-standing systems of behavior deserve to remain in existence because they are established traditions? | 165 |
| 45 | Have modern advancements improved the quality of people's lives? | 168 |
| 46 | Are politicians, by virtue of being public figures, under pressure to succeed? | 172 |
| 47 | Can fame be the bearer of happiness, or are people who are not famous more likely to be happy? | 178 |
| 48 | Is the world changing for the better? | 183 |
| 49 | A conscience is a powerful motivator, but is it more influential than money, fame or power? | 186 |
| 50 | Are the greatest griefs in life those that we cause ourselves? | 189 |
| 51 | Does effort lead to success more than luck? | 193 |

| 52 | What qualities define heroism and courage? | 197 |
| 53 | Does fame contribute to happiness? | 200 |
| 54 | Does the public expect too much from public figures? | 204 |
| 55 | Does struggle make us value our success and achievements? | 208 |
| 56 | Does the current system of education promote the acquisition of knowledge, or does it persuade students to conceal their lack of knowledge? | 212 |
| 57 | Should the gas emissions of nation states be tracked by an international monitoring organization? | 217 |
| 58 | Does a strong desire for technological attainment cause a society to neglect other values, such as education and the protection of the environment? | 222 |
| 59 | Should the government take responsibility for making sure that people lead healthy lives? | 226 |
| 60 | Should people adopt new ideas or values instead of relying on tradition? | 230 |

LIKE TEST PREP

# Write a Test Essay in 25 Min.

1. Time yourself with a countdown watch or a stopwatch. When you cannot finish within the given time limit, mark it. Give yourself enough time to finish your essay. Practice writing essays this way.

2. Outline before you write an essay. Write an essay only when you have a good outline. A good outline contains a persuasive argument, compelling supports, and three or more historical/literary examples. Ask your writing tutor to give you comments on the appropriateness of the examples or quotes in your outlines and essays.

3. Get your essays scored and corrected on the use of vocabulary, grammar, punctuation, and organization by a writing tutor. Ask him/her to score your essay each time you submit a revision. Revise until you get a score above 8 out of 12 total. If you feel like you need a higher standard, set 10 out of 12 for a passing paper.

4. Practice rewriting the revised essay until you know how to write it blindfolded. Practice writing it within 22-23 minutes. Then, give yourself 2-3 minutes to review what you wrote before you submit it. Once you have one great essay, you can apply your knowledge (vocabulary, expressions, and examples, and arguments) and skills (essay organization skills and the ability to write a quality essay within the given time) in writing other essays.

5. Practice rephrasing the sentences from your reading and model essays. Circle the words or expressions you would like to learn. Create new sentences with them. You can look up the dictionary or ask your writing tutor to help you with them.

6. There are a lot of similar topics on essay tests. Get a list of commonly appearing essay topics and categorize the most common ones together so that you can apply the same logic and examples on similar essay topics.

7. Practice outlining in your mind with the common test essay topics. You may take notes as you think of arguments and examples.

1. Argument

2. Support 1: 1-2 examples

3. Support 1: 1-2 examples

4. Support 1: 1-2 examples or Counter-argument: examples

5. Concluding Statement

If you can come up with a good outline in five or six sentences in 3-5 minutes, consider yourself quite successful.

# HOW TO WRITE A TEST ESSAY -THE APPEARANCE

Your Test essay should look like a four or five paragraph essay with a clear introduction, body and a conclusion. We suggest four or five paragraphs because you need to provide more than two examples and one body paragraph is not enough for that. In terms of length, make sure you fill out both pages given to you.

Your essay represents you. Write in good handwriting and try not make a mess on your paper. If your essay is neat and orderly, that's what you are to them as the essay graders don't know your name, gender, age, or the school you attend. They only see you on paper. They can only make assumptions.

Also remember that your essay is scored holistically, meaning that the essay graders scores your essay based on its overall impression. They have a score in mind as they read it. They are trained to give an essay a 4 or a 5. You want to give your essay graders a favorable impression, right?

Introduction
Body 1-support 1
Body 2-support 2
Body 3-support 3or Counter-argument
Conclusion

Introduction
Body 1-compare/contrast or advantages/disadvantages
Body 2- compare/contrast or advantages/disadvantages
Conclusion

# HOW TO WRITE A TEST ESSAY -THE OVERALL STRUCTURE

Paragraph one is the introduction. You may start your essay with a famous/relevant quote to the topic that only educated people know and can recognize that you are smart, although your readers don't know everybody and every literature on the planet. Do not ramble on with pointless some people say this and others say that. Focus on presenting a clear and thoughtful argument backed up by strong supports. Don't be wishy-washy and swing like a pendulum. You can enumerate them (e.g. first, second, third). Your introduction should be a guide through your essay.

Start the second paragraph with a topic sentence. and then provide specific examples from history, literature, and current events. Provide dates and names of incidents and people. Be accurate. You can end your second paragraph or give a preview your third paragraph.

Start the third paragraph with a topic sentence. and then provide specific examples from history, literature, and current events. Provide dates and names of incidents and people. Be accurate. You can end your third paragraph or give a preview your fourth paragraph.

Start the fourth paragraph with a topic sentence. and then provide specific examples from history, literature, and current events. Provide dates and names of incidents and people. Be accurate.

In your conclusion, you can summarize what you said in your essay and make a conclusion. If the content and the logic of your body paragraphs were rich and convincing, you would find it easy writing this part. Don't be too specific like you were in the body paragraphs as it is time to end your argument. Be general. You may end with a quote if you want but try not to abuse them.

| | | | | | |
|---|---|---|---|---|---|
| Length | no conclusion | Less Than 1 Page | 1 Page | 1 & 1/2 Page | 2 Pages |
| Language | Poor | Fair Spoken Slang Cliché | Average Simple | Good Flowery Redundant | Excellent Abstraction Academic & Neutral |
| Grammar | Poor | Fair | Average | Good | Excellent |
| Spelling & Punctuation | Poor | Fair | Average | Good | Excellent |
| Organization | Poor | Fair | Average Formulaic | Good | Excellent |
| Examples | Irrelevant | Relevant but not specific | Hypothetical | Personal | Historical Current Literary |
| Creativity | Poor | Fair | Average Formulaic | Good | Excellent |
| Argument | Poor Absolute Claim Irrelevant | Fair | Average | Good | Excellent counter-argument |
| Content | Off-Topic Poor | Poor | Fair | Average | Excellent |
| Clarity | Poor | Fair | Average | Good | Excellent |
| Persuasiveness | Poor | Fair | Average | Good | Excellent |
| Handwriting | Poor | Fair | Average | Good | Excellent |

# HOW TO WRITE A TEST ESSAY -ADVANCED WRITING SCORING RUBRIC

This table shows you what you need in your essay for a high score. Try to avoid the problems on the left side: stay on the right. You will do well.

# HOW TO WRITE A TEST ESSAY -THE OUTLINE

1. argument

2~3. at least 2 supports 1-2 examples each

4. argument+why

1. Argument:: We can benefit from learning about the flaws of famous figures.

2. Support 1: We can learn from the achievements of famous people, and nobody is perfect ex) Achilles, Hercules, Odysseus, Hector, Alexander the Great, Princess Diana, JFK all had personal flaws.

3. Support 2: We don't make the same mistakes as the famous people did. ex) We don't have to live miserable lives like Sylvia Plath/Virginia Wolf.

4. Counter-argument: However, not all famous people's flaws are acceptable or valuable. ex) H. Truman using the atomic bomb in Hiroshima on civilians to stop WWII is unacceptable just like Hitler and Churchill cannot be excused from the blame of attacking the innocent civilians.

5. Thesis: Important lessons can be learned from the flaws of famous people without risking our lives or precious resources. (argument+why).

# HOW TO WRITE A TEST ESSAY -THE INTRODUCTION

There are myriad ways to write an essay, but here I suggest two. Try to imitate these until you develop your own style. Sample 1 ends with a thoughtful argument, and Sample 2 ends with a preview of the body. Try not to go too specific and try not to use examples in the introduction.

## Sample 1

Intro-The discovery that someone we admire has done something wrong is always disappointing and disillusioning. Yet even when people we consider heroes have been tarnished by their faults, they are no less valuable than people who appear perfect. <u>When we learn that an admired person, even one who is seemingly perfect, has behaved in less than admirable ways, we discover a complex truth: great ideas and great deeds come from imperfect people like ourselves.</u>

## Sample 2

Intro-Changing decisions when circumstances change is often better than sticking to the original plan. Living in human society, people are often expected to stick to their original plans to be consistent. <u>However, one needs to be flexible in order to wisely adapt to fast changing situations.</u> Examples can be given in the cases of Ralph Waldo Emerson, Bertrand Russell, and Vladimir Lenin.

Body-Emerson in his _____ essay argued that one does not need to be consistent.

# HOW TO WRITE A TEST ESSAY -THE BODY

1. Try to use as many abstractions and nominalizations (big words) as possible. Try to hit the nail at once with that one word instead of beating around the bushes.
(an equal opportunity policy that allows a certain percentage of colored students to be admitted to schools that serves public: <u>affirmative action</u>) (sentencing someone to death: <u>capital punishment</u>) (right to vote: <u>suffrage</u>) (protesting without violent behavior: <u>non-violent passive resistance</u>) (human beings are free from destiny or God's plans: <u>free will</u>) (depending on each other: <u>interdependence</u>)

2. Avoid overused expressions. Substitute simple words with difficult one.
(many->plethora) (attend->matriculate) (cry->lament) (cause->induce) (ignore->disdain) (to do list->agenda) (change->enhance or redirect) (honorable->dignified) (instead of->as an alternative to) (end->pull out of) (think of->devise)

3. Use nominalizations instead of simple verbs.
(prefer->preference) (disturb->deter->deterrence)

4. Use educated expressions, examples, and quotations from few famous people that is applicable in many different situations and practice using them.
(Descartes' "<u>cogito ergo sum</u>": I think, therefore I exist) (<u>a priori</u>: before) (<u>magnum opus</u>: a masterpiece) (<u>mens rea</u>: guilty mind) (<u>albeit</u>: in spite of) (<u>tabula rasa</u>: an empty table)

5. Try to connect your body paragraphs. Build good transitions so that your ideas flow from one to another more smoothly (See Sample 2 on page v.)

Here, two body paragraphs are given as an example. The author starts with a clear topic sentence (one of the most…) at the beginning of the body paragraph. The specific names mentioned (World War I, Fritz Haber, "father of chemical warfare," Media Awareness Network (2010)) gives power and authority to the essay.

Also note that the transition (In addition…) between body paragraphs is smooth as the second paragraph can use the first paragraph as a support to further discuss the topic. <u>Use proper quotations or at least make your essay sound like you are quoting an important person or media.</u>

## Sample Body

<u>One of the most detrimental effects of technology is how it makes war more violent and destructive</u>. For example, one of the reasons why <u>World War I</u> was one of the deadliest conflicts of all time is because we were able to manufacture many fatal weapons by utilizing improved technology. During this war, combatants expanded the use of catastrophic armaments, such as machine guns, combat planes and tanks. These deadly machines were made possible by <u>the application of scientific knowledge</u> developed by scientists, including a Dutch chemist, <u>Fritz Haber.</u> He used his knowledge to introduce chlorine gas, earning him the "father of chemical warfare" title.

<u>In addition</u>, violence can be generated by exposure to diverse media, such as television and the internet, which are
also products of technology. <u>Media Awareness Network (2010) argues that</u> naive young people can be harmed by identifying themselves with brutality displayed in the media. This demonstrates that technology not only affects the global village, but may also increase aggression in people.

# HOW TO WRITE A TEST ESSAY -THE CONCLUSION

Rephrase and summarize in your conclusion. You can reopen your conclusion with a general statement. Then summarize your specific points that you discussed in the body paragraphs. Make a concluding statement which incorporates your statements. Do not discuss anything specifically or suggest examples in this section. <u>Do not talk about any arguments, supports, or examples that you did not mention in the body paragraphs.</u> Be concise and stay focused.

Sample Conclusion

While we enjoy the convenience and advancements made possible by the development of technology, we must not overlook the side effects of the process. In order to assure our future existence and to prevent cataclysmal events, governments around the globe must devise plans to cope with problems facing mankind. <u>Perhaps the most crucial task humankind has to implement is to ex-cogitate an eclectic solution that will allow us to reap the benefits of technology, while not being overwhelmed by its negative aspects.</u>

> 1. Are actions more important to consider than people's intentions?

It is very important to try to understand people's motivations before judging their actions. Egregious, outrageous behavior may appear to stem from innate evilness but there are factors in play that are not perceptible to outsiders. A person may appear harmful and inconsiderate but perhaps the person was confronted with extraneous circumstances. People should always try to understand why people act the way they do.

Understanding other people is far more important than indicting people through a moral framework. The founding of psychology as a discipline came after that of religion and is an evolutionary offshoot of many moral philosophies. Instead of judging people through black and white moral notions, evil and good, bad and good, the primary focus of psychology is to understand the inner workings of the mind.

Nietzsche, in his *Genealogy of Morality*, claimed that there is no fixed moral universe, and that morality itself is subject to change according to culture. With the discipline of psychology and some moral philosophies in mind, it can be said that the nature of a strange individual cannot be encapsulated with narrow words such as inconsiderate, harmful, and evil.

Moving away from the sciences and philosophy, there are factors in play that are not observable by outside parties. For example, a village may consider a local boy as absolutely contemptible because he steals bread from bakers, and puts on his back stolen clothes hung on a clothesline by neighbors. But upon closer inspection, this very child may come from a broken home with little supervision from his guardians who failed to teach him basic ethics. Indeed with the case of this neighborhood thief, a moral indictment is less prudent than attempting to understand the upbringing of the child.

Moreover, there is a sense of permanence when pronouncing a certain moral or personal attribute onto others. People change, and therefore personality descriptors should hardly be used to judge others. A sentence of judgment is a finality to the object being judged. However harmful, inconsiderate, outrageous personality traits will more than likely undergo change. Inconsideration of others may have been a psychological reaction to being taken advantage of by friends and acquaintances. As soon as this outlook on peo ple is adjusted, so does the inconsideration to people. Therefore, pronouncing a fixed judgment on a person is far from dependable.

In conclusion, it is best not to judge people according to hindsight evaluations of their actions. There are many factors leading people to act the way they do. Moreover because people change, and pronouncing judgment is a sort of final opinion to the issue, it is best to rely on science and psychology when making personality assumptions.

## Model Sentences of Essay # 1

1. Egregious, outrageous behavior may appear to stem from innate evilness but there are factors in play that are not perceptible to outsiders.

2. A person may appear harmful and inconsiderate but perhaps the person was confronted with extraneous circumstances.

3. The founding of psychology as a discipline came after that of religion and is an evolutionary offshoot of many moral philosophies.

4. Nietzsche, in his Genealogy of Morality, claimed that there is no fixed moral universe, and that morality itself is subject to change according to culture.

5. With the discipline of psychology and some moral philosophies in mind, it can be said that the nature of a strange individual cannot be encapsulated with narrow words such as inconsiderate, harmful, and evil.

6. For example, a village may consider a local boy as absolutely contemptible because he steals bread from bakers, and puts on his back stolen clothes hung on a clothesline by neighbors.

7. People change, and therefore personality descriptors should hardly be used to judge others.

8. Moreover because people change, and pronouncing judgment is a sort of final opinion to the issue, it is best to rely on science and psychology when making personality assumptions.

2. Which is better for society: when its members simply follow the ideas of leaders or when its members act as individuals?

A society with limited restrictions on the expression of ideas and opinions is better off than a society with a propensity to censor. A society does not reach its full potential socially, culturally, and economically when members of society are threatened for being truthful.

Evidence shows that healthy democracies have within their nation-state boundaries a vibrant press and media. In contrast, societies that are steeped in paranoia, which are typically operated from under a tyrannical state and by a dictatorship, are bankrupt from the sort of mechanisms that lead people to openly share their opinions on art, politics, lifestyle choices, and mutual interests commonly seen among societies with a free and open press.

A society with people who incessantly copy the ideas and opinions of others are typically under external pressure to do so, and as a result of such insipid social imitation, the rate of social, economic, and cultural development that would otherwise transpire in a free and open society is weak. A society composed of men and women who are not bound by popular convention is a society - when coupled with p ositive economic factors – with the most amount of happiness.

There is a measurable improvement in overall social happiness when certain members of any given society is allowed to express their unique ideas. Since all societies, open or not open, have conventions on what is appropriate and not appropriate, what is true and not true, it is still important that societies allow outlier members to deviate from convention.

As soon as the deviation from medium social behavior is not allowed, there is a measurable decline in overall social happiness, as there are certain members who are being censored and affected unfavorably. Moreover, the historical pattern has shown that free and open societies develop at a faster and healthier rate. A society is structurally unsound when members of society copy the ideas and opinions of others.

When George Orwell released 1984, the threat of communism was a very real threat to the West. The book painted a picture of a society with limited freedom to express. As a result, this Orwellian society suffered in its production of the arts, literature, and economic development. Expressionism was so stifled that the press officer of the republi c, Senior Mellenieuv, went unchallenged as he mandated the discontinuation of the color purple from the spectrum of colors. Indeed, in this Orwellian society, the fact that members of society copied the idea that the color purple does not exist, signified that the society was structurally unsound due to the authoritarian government.

It is not necessary to cite Orwellian, dystopian societies when there are modern-day examples. Contemporary nation-states with a long track record of human rights violations often stifle the freedom to express ideas and opinions. Take, for example, the current crisis in Syria: President Bashar is carrying out a violent crackdown on protesters who are merely expressing their opinion on the current government of their country.

Although being natural born citizens, these protesters are not allowed to express their opinions. As a result, there are fierce conflicts transpiring in Syria. Contemporary Syria is a case where lack of individuality and freedom to express has enraged a segment of the population, causing internal strife, and economic depression. The society of Syria is structurally unsound as long as there are individuals who must copy the ideas and opinions of others in order to remain safe.

In conclusion, society is better off when individuals are allowed to interact and express without persecution. As soon as fear is used to pressure individuals to contain individualism, society as a whole stumbles developmentally. A free and open society has the highest amount of happiness, and such prosperity is reflected by its economic, cultural, and political development.

## Model Sentences of Essay # 2

1. A society with limited restrictions on the expression of ideas and opinions is better off than a society with a propensity to censor.

2. Evidence shows that healthy democracies have within their nation-state boundaries a vibrant press and media.

3. In contrast, societies that are steeped in paranoia, which are typically operated from under a tyrannical state and by a dictatorship, are bankrupt from the sort of mechanisms that lead people to openly share their opinions on art, politics, lifestyle choices, and mutual interests commonly seen among societies with a free and open press.

4. Since all societies, open or not open, have conventions on what is appropriate and not appropriate, what is true and not true, it is still important that societies allow outlier members to deviate from convention.

5. Contemporary nation-states with a long track record of human rights violations often stifle the freedom to express ideas and opinions.

6. A society composed of men and women who are not bound by popular convention is a society - when coupled with positive economic factors – with the most amount of happiness.

7. Contemporary Syria is a case where lack of individuality and freedom to express has enraged a segment of the population, causing internal strife, and economic depression.

8. As soon as fear is used to pressure individuals to contain individualism, society as a whole stumbles developmentally.

9. A free and open society has the highest amount of happiness, and such prosperity is reflected by its economic, cultural, and political development.

10. The society of Syria is structurally unsound as long as there are individuals who must copy the ideas and opinions of others in order to remain safe.

> 3. Are mainstream views and ideas more likely to be valid?

The truth and facts have little to no correlation to what is popular or mainstream. Although human nature seeks the truth, it is also succumbs to dubious information for a variety of reasons. There are instances in which false information gives comfort to people or provides physical safety from provocateurs, making them forego basic logic.

Since people have only the observation of natural phenomena and the scientific method and, finally, each other to validate their claims, it is often the case that the nodding of heads is sufficient for false information to become the conventional idea. As history shows, widely held views often have a shelf life, being popular for affected generations until a watershed event or scientific breakthrough causes people to question widely held beliefs and dogma.

Prescribed doctrine proclaimed as unquestionably true by a particular group is a sort of religious dogma. Conversely, when challenging the unquestionable, there are consequences, especially in societies where certain widespread tenets are held dangerously sacred. In the case of ideas where views are not to be challenged, many people, although na turally predisposed to seek the truth, will tap into their first instinct to survive and therefore revert to what is safe to say. Here safety is more important than communicating the truth. There is ample evidence in history to suggest that fear and persecution compel people to accept the unreasonable as fact.

The inquisition in Early-Modern Spain is a striking example on how fear of persecution compelled many to abstain from science and philosophy. Although many early-modern European artists and writers traced their birth to the Iberian Peninsula, Northern Europeans associated the region with "the black legend." The black legend finds its most usual expression, that is, its typical form, in judgments about cruelty, superstition, and political tyranny. Aside from the construed cruelty and political tyranny of the Spanish government towards native peoples in the Americas, catholic dogma and superstition rampant among the Spanish population caused many Northern Europeans to believe the peninsula opposed the spiritual progress and intellectual activity of the North.

Catholic Europe is an example on how religious dogma, being the widespread belief among the population, lagged the population behind the North in scientific achievem ents and human rights. For example, when the Italian astronomer, Galileo, defended the tenets of Heliocentricism, believing that the Sun was the center of the solar system not the Earth, the Catholic administration in Italy persecuted him. Christian scripture at the time was taken literally.

In the instance of Galileo's trial, the biblical reference, Psalm 104:5, which says "the Lord set the earth on its foundations; it can never be moved" was cited as evidence against what would become a commonly known fact, that the Earth is indeed not the center of the universe. The persecution of Galileo by the widespread belief that the Earth was indeed the center of the universe is a striking example in history on how common held beliefs are not always correct.

In conclusion, the truth and facts often do not reflect what is popular. People nod their heads to common beliefs for a variety of reasons. Many times, people believe in widely held beliefs in order to remain safe, despite whether the beliefs are commonsensical.

## Model Sentences of Essay # 3

1. The truth and facts have little to no correlation with what is popular or mainstream.

2. Although human nature seeks the truth, it is also succumbs to dubious information for a variety of reasons.

3. There are instances in which false information gives comfort to people or provides physical safety from provocateurs, making them forego basic logic.

4. Since people have only the observation of natural phenomena and the scientific method and, finally, each other to validate their claims, it is often the case that the nodding of heads is sufficient for false information to become the conventional idea.

5. As history shows, widely held views often have a shelf life, being popular for affected generations until a watershed event or scientific breakthrough causes people to question widely held beliefs and dogma.

6. Conversely, when challenging the unquestionable, there are consequences, especially in societies where certain widespread tenets are held dangerously sacred.

7. In the case of ideas where views are not to be challenged, many people, although naturally predisposed to seek the truth, will tap into their first instinct to survive and therefore revert to what is safe to say.

8. The inquisition in Early-Modern Spain is a striking example on how fear of persecution compelled many to abstain from science and philosophy.

9. Catholic Europe is an example on how religious dogma, being the widespread belief among the population, lagged the population behind the North in scientific achievements and human rights.

10. The persecution of Galileo by the widespread belief that the Earth was indeed the center of the universe is a striking example in history on how common held beliefs are not always correct.

## 4. Is it better for people to be realistic or optimistic?

I think being realistic is better than being headlessly optimistic. It is more advantageous to understand the facts and obstacles of any given action or goal taken than being optimistic and thereby headstrong and dreamy. Although it can be said that realistic people lack long term goals and are short sighted, the reverse can be said about optimistic people. The latter group does not have the proper perspective to achieve short term goals in order to eventually reach their lofty, long term goals. Realistic people have in their mental arsenal the ability to get short term goals completed, allowing them to, inch by inch, reach loftier goals mirroring the optimists.

One reason why being a realist is better than being an optimist, is because facts and the situation at hand is far more important than simply wishing a desirable outcome. Realists are closely related to pragmatists. William James, the father of Pragmatism, espoused the practical approach to problems and affairs. Pragmatists are more concerned with how to get from A to B, and then from B to C, and so forth, than are the optimists. Hypothetically, optimists may desire greatly to reach destination C, but have no sense of pragmatism to conquer A and B first.

Furthermore optimists are too headstrong. It is a sign of measurable intelligence when a laboratory animal thrown into a skinner's box, being tested on positive and negative stimuli, stops electrocution by repeating the same action. In a sense the dreamy optimist is similar to a non-sentient laboratory animal, clicking repeatedly on a button without knowing what will transpire immediately thereafter. The realist, being a cousin of the pragmatist, is most concerned with the immediate consequence of an action.

In conclusion, there are many advantages to being realistic, and many disadvantages to being optimistic. Realists understand the facts and obstacles and therefore often make informed decisions. On the other hand, optimists are too headstrong and dreamy and therefore make many mistakes, and continue to make them without veering from their course.

## Model Sentences of Essay # 4

1. Although it can be said that realistic people lack long term goals and are short sighted, the reverse can be said about optimistic people.

2. The latter group does not have the proper perspective to achieve short-term goals in order to eventually reach their lofty, long term goals.

3. Realistic people have in their mental arsenal the ability to get short term goals completed, allowing them to, inch by inch, reach loftier goals mirroring the optimists.

4. In a sense the dreamy optimist is similar to a non-sentient laboratory animal, clicking repeatedly on a button without knowing what will transpire immediately afterwards.

5. The realist, being a cousin of the pragmatist, is most concerned with the immediate consequence of an action.

6. On the other hand, optimists are too headstrong and dreamy and therefore make many mistakes, and continue to make them without veering from their course.

7. Realists understand the facts and obstacles and therefore often make informed decisions.

Optimists are too headstrong and dreamy and therefore make many mistakes, and continue to make them without veering from their course.

> 5. Should government employ everything at its disposal to protect citizens?

The function and the role of the government has been debated upon for ages without any concrete answer being offered as to how much is exactly enough or even too much. Especially with today's so-called declaration of "War on Terror," we have witnessed a pre-emptive war, aggression inflicted in the name of national security as an unavoidable misfortune practiced by a government in order to protect its citizens.

Although such political situations are far from being simple, what seems clear is the necessity for a type of utilitarian perspective that is neither totalitarian nor xenophobic. A government shall never exercise absolute power no matter what the point of justification may be, for the possibility of ill consequence is too great.

The reason why fear is perhaps the supreme apparatus of political propaganda is that fear naturally induces the need for security, and thus, it could be utilized as a powerful agent for governmental control. Limitations on freedom and individual rights deceptively come as an inevitable sacrifice that is first said to apply only to the accused or the "oth er." As citizens first do not believe that the tightened grip applies to them personally, they are willing to forgo their civil liberties for that heightened sense of security. However, what they do not realize at that moment is that once the legal device is put into place, the classification of inclusivity remains flexible.

We have witnessed this to be true countless times. The fact that wartime sacrifices civil liberties simply illustrates this. In the time of war, logic, reason, and compassion, all characteristics usually heralded as the epitome of humanity often fail to apply. Consequently, in the time of insecurity, the prime role of government becomes the protection of its citizens through any means necessary, which by definition transcends any "boundary" in the legal sense of the term.

George Washington, one of the founding fathers, as a matter of fact, the first President of the United States, keenly warned us of the delicate role of the government for "government is not reason; it is not eloquent; it is force. Like fire, it is a dangerous servant and a fearful master." And thus, like fire, it should always be kept on a close watch and a careful distance, for if the heat of the patriotic flame were to ever get too extreme, the almost invisible haze of smoke will blind our sight from recognizing even our own sister.

## Model Sentences of Essay # 5

1. The function and the role of the government has been debated upon for ages without any concrete answer being offered as to how much is exactly enough or even too much.

2. Especially with today's so-called declaration of "War on Terror," we have witnessed a pre-emptive war, aggression inflicted in the name of national security as an unavoidable misfortune practiced by a government in order to protect its citizens.

3. Although such political situations are far from being simple, what seems clear is the necessity for a type of utilitarian perspective that is neither totalitarian nor xenophobic.

4. The reason why fear is perhaps the supreme apparatus of political propaganda is that fear naturally induces the need for security, and thus, it could be utilized as a powerful agent for governmental control.

5. Limitations on freedom and individual rights deceptively come as an inevitable sacrifice that is first said to apply only to the accused or the "other."

6. As citizens first do not believe that the tightened grip applies to them personally, they are willing to forgo their civil liberties for that heightened sense of security.

7. However, what they do not realize at that moment is that once the legal device is put into place, the classification of inclusivity remains flexible.

> 6. Are some dreams worth the ultimate price – death?

Dreams can go beyond a career choice and material desires. They can relate to belief systems. Of course, dreams are worth dying for if they have been examined closely and are based on a foundation of justice and righteousness.

Today, for example, South Korean armed forces face a situation that tests their commitment to democracy and freedom - and that could lead to their untimely deaths. So, the lives and dreams of South Korean military forces, along with the citizens they are defending, are on the line.

Indeed, tensions remain high on the Korean peninsula after the recent North Korean artillery attack on South Korea's Yeonpyeong Island that left four South Koreans dead and nearly 20 injured. And some top South Korean officials, including Won Sei-hoon, the chief of the National Intelligence Service, believe that North Korea will likely attack again.

With the possibility of war on the horizon, South Korean forces must again ask themselves whether they are willing to die for democracy and freedom. Such deliberations must go beyond mere nationalism and defending one's cou ntry. Human rights are at issue. North Korea has a totalitarian form of government that subjugates the human rights and well-being of its people. Friedrich Durrenmatt, the late Swiss novelist, told us what's necessary to protect human rights: "Only the freedom of mind can prevent the state from becoming totalitarian and from issuing totalitarian demands."

At the risk of being overly sentimental, it remains profound to say freedom is a human right and should be protected with death if necessary. So, yes, dreams are worth dying for if they have been analyzed and understood. South Korea's military service members and citizens are in harm's way. And, they have dreams indelibly tied to freedom. Those dreams may soon come face to face with, and be tested by, the North Koreans.

Model Sentences of Essay # 6

1. Dreams can go beyond a career choice and material desires.

2. Dreams are worth dying for if they have been examined closely and are based on a foundation of justice and righteousness.

3. South Korean armed forces face a situation that tests their commitment to democracy and freedom - and that could lead to their untimely deaths.

4. With the possibility of war on the horizon, South Korean forces must again ask themselves whether they are willing to die for their democracy and freedom.

5. Such deliberations must go beyond mere nationalism and defending one's country.

6. North Korea has a totalitarian form of government that subjugates the human rights and well-being of its people.

7. At the risk of being overly sentimental, it remains profound to say freedom is a human right and should be protected with death if necessary.

8. Indeed, tensions remain high on the Korean peninsula after the recent North Korean artillery attack on South Korea's Yeonpyeong Island that left four South Koreans dead and nearly 20 injured.

> 7. Should education emphasize creativity as much as literacy and mathematics?

These days, the purpose of education these days seems to be a straightforward one: to equip the student with the tools to be a financial success. Making money and gaining status are the twin goals of our materialistic society. Of course, being a success socially and financially is a worthy thing; we all have to eat, and we would all like to enjoy the benefits of prosperity. However, the soul craves self-expression more than money, and schools should and must promote creativity.

To begin with, the world is currently suffering the effects of a money-above-all culture. Financial institutions around the globe have collapsed as a result of the blind pursuit of profit by money managers, stockbrokers, and banks. The Bible says, "The love of money is the root of all evil." Money is good, but meaning is better. Making our way in the world, finding what we were meant to do and what brings us happiness, is what leads to a happy life. Happy people make others happy, too, and one painting or poem can tell us more about the meaning of life than a thousand spreadsheets.

The famous American psychologist Abraham Maslow found that, once certain basic needs (such as food, shelter, and safety) are met, the amount of income someone has is no predictor of happiness. Millionaires are as likely to be miserable as 40-hour-a-week office workers. Rather, the highest goal of humans is self-actualization. That is, people need to express their hopes, fears, dreams, and talents. Schools need to encourage dance, poetry, sculpture, and as many methods of self-expression as they can, in order to produce happy, productive, creative graduates ready to share their gifts to the world.

Our school systems need to encourage students to use every form of thought they're capable of producing. Sir Ken says, "We think about the world in all the ways that we experience it. We think visually, we think in sound, we think kinesthetically, we think in abstract terms, we think in movement." Only by using all of their talents can people become all they are meant to be. Those who have the most talent in the fields favored by traditional education, such as science and mathematics, will still rise to the top.

In the final analysis, traditional education has brought the world to the state it's in today. If we want an overcrowded, overheated world in conflict, we should keep doing w hat we have been doing in our schools. However, if we want a sane, humane, creative world full of possibilities, we need to follow Sir Ken's advice and encourage our children's talents. They will blossom like flowers and fill the world with their colors.

## Model Sentences of Essay # 7

1. Financial institutions around the globe have collapsed as a result of the blind pursuit of profit by money managers, stockbrokers, and banks.

2. The famous American psychologist Abraham Maslow found that, once certain basic needs (such as food, shelter, and safety) are met, the amount of income someone has is no predictor of happiness.

3. Millionaires are as likely to be miserable as 40-hour-a-week office workers.

4. Schools need to encourage dance, poetry, sculpture, and as many methods of self-expression as they can, in order to produce happy, productive, creative graduates ready to share their gifts to the world.

5. Our school systems need to encourage students to use every form of thought they're capable of producing.

6. However, if we want a sane, humane, creative world full of possibilities, we need to follow Sir Ken's advice and encourage our children's talents.

7. They will blossom like flowers and fill the world with their colors.

## 8. Is happiness the result of one's decision to be content in life?

The greater part of our happiness or misery indeed depends on our dispositions and not our circumstances. It may be in fact that our circumstances themselves may be determined by our state of mind, so better emotions lead to improved circumstances.

First, we must acknowledge that there are certainly circumstances that cannot be altered simply by happy thoughts. An individual on a sinking ship needs to find a lifeboat, and this reality will not be changed by positive thinking. However, this may of course be considered an emergency situation, not something that people face on a daily basis. For the person in more mundane circumstances, a positive attitude will go a long ways towards consistent happiness.

Secondly, we have examples from history as evidence. The trials of Job eventually led to the restoration of his family and wealth to a degree he had never seen before. One man, over the course of 28 years lost his job, failed twice in business, failed several times to win elections, and had a nervous breakdown. In 1860, Abraham Lincoln was elected president of the United States. Thomas Edison is well k nown for failing primary school, resorting to home schooling by his mother, but he is even more famous for the inventions that these successes became.

It's difficult to gauge whether these successes equate to happiness or misery, there is unfortunately no shortage of miserable successful men. Some of these arguably successful individuals were indeed content and happy with their life, but others were not happy and in fact, they were miserable and depressed. Their success could not curtail the happiness or lack of happiness produced by their disposition.

A friend of motivational and business speaker Robert J Ringer bears this out. His friend retired, and began making stained glass lamps as a way to pass the time. After doing this for several months, he found himself on the beach one day, and a feeling of utter contentment washed over him. Sadly it lasted only a short period. With the success in making, and then selling his lamps, he found himself hiring employees, dealing with accounting, and back in the same rat race he had retired from. His friend briefly found solace and happiness, and then, in pursuing more income by opening a business, the entrepreneur no longer felt satisfied with life.

Finally, it is obvious that emotions such as happiness

are to a large part under our control. A person has the ability to take a set of circumstances into consideration and choose his emotional response for better or for worse. Martha Washington speaks the truth when she says that happiness or misery is dependent on our disposition, and not or circumstances.

## Model Sentences of Essay # 8

1. The greater part of our happiness or misery depends on our dispositions and not our circumstances.

2. An individual on a sinking ship needs to find a lifeboat, and positive thinking will not change this reality.

3. Thomas Edison is well known for failing primary school, resorting to home schooling by his mother, but he is even more famous for the inventions that these successes became.

4. It's difficult to gauge whether these successes equate to happiness or misery, there is unfortunately no shortage of miserable successful men.

5. Some of these arguably successful individuals were indeed content and happy with their life, but others were not happy and in fact, they were miserable and depressed.

6. With the success in making, and then selling his lamps, he found himself hiring employees, dealing with accounting, and back in the same rat race he had retired from.

7. His friend briefly found solace and happiness, and then, in pursuing more income by opening a business, the entrepreneur no longer felt satisfied with life.

8. Finally, it is obvious that emotions such as happiness are to a large part under our control.

## 9. Which is more important to the international community: the nation-state or the individual?

Between the nation-state and the individual, the nation-state is the most important symbol to the international community. Although there are international monitoring agencies with the sole objective of overseeing human rights issues, the rights of people are second to the geopolitical situation of nations. Put in another way, the nation-state dominates the spotlight while individuals receive disproportionately less attention. The distribution of power within the United Nations will be analyzed to decipher whether the nation-state as a political entity receives more attention than individuals.

The organization that measures the international pulse is the United Nations. Created immediately after the Second World War, the organization is a collaboration of global nations sharing common interests such as global stability and peace. Individuals representing their nations are ranked and ordered by the country of which they represent. Despite being called the United Nations, the organization is not egalitarian in its distribution of power and representative voting power. The United Nations does not allocate equita ble powers to Nations according to their global share of the human population, but instead the paradigm of power within the organization is based on economic, historical, and military factors.

Although there are One hundred and ninety-six countries, only five nations dominate the United Nations. Only the United States, Russia, China, France, and England have veto powers that can overturn the majority opinion of other nations. Aside from China and the United States, the security council has a relatively low population count compared to nations such as India, Indonesia, Brazil, and even Nigeria. If individuals were a more important symbol to the international community, then countries with a larger amount of people would naturally command more authority in the United Nations.

The historical, economic, and military situation of demographically large nations following the Second World War, are the reasons for their lack of power in the United Nations. The economic order in 1945 was firmly concentrated in the West, with the exception of Japan. The economic power of nations closely related to their military capacity, as advanced weaponry and ability to mobilize hundreds of thousands of soldiers required a strong industrial base. Wit h a massive population dwarfing the European powers combined, the sub-continent and ancient civilization of India did not become a Security Council member because of its weak industrial economy and colonial tributary status. The economic and military power of nations was not the only factor in the years following World War II.

With the case of Japan, a telling prerequisite for demanding more power in the United Nations was the political situation of nations. Defeated nations aligned with Nazi Germany were automatically denied entrance, leaving Italy, Japan, and West and East Germany, great economic and military powers, out of the running. Indeed, the structure of the United Nations, the great symbol of International cooperation, was designed by a group of militarily battered nations after World War II.

In conclusion, it is more likely that nation-states receive more attention from the media and powerful organizations than do individuals. The symbol of international consensus and pulse, the United Nations, awards more power and authority to nations based on their economic, military, and historical circumstances than their demographic situation. If individuals were more important and symbolic to the international community than nation-states, then nations wit h larger populations would command a proportionate amount of power in the United Nations.

<u>Model Sentences of Essay # 9</u>

1. Although there are international monitoring agencies with the sole objective of overseeing human rights issues, the rights of people are second to the geopolitical situation of nations.

2. The distribution of power within the United Nations will be analyzed to decipher whether the nation-state as a political entity receives more attention than individuals.

3. Created immediately after the Second World War, the organization is a collaboration of global nations sharing common interests such as global stability and peace.

4. Individuals representing their nations are ranked and ordered by the country of which they represent.

5. Aside from China and the United States, the security council has a relatively low population count compared to nations such as India, Indonesia, Brazil, and even Nigeria.

6. If individuals were a more important symbol to the international community, then countries with a larger amount of people would naturally command more authority in the United Nations.

7. The economic power of nations closely related to their military capacity, as advanced weaponry and ability to mobilize hundreds of thousands of soldiers required a strong industrial base.

8. With a massive population dwarfing the European powers combined, the sub-continent and ancient

civilization of India did not become a Security Council member because of its weak industrial economy and colonial tributary status.

9. The symbol of international consensus and pulse, the United Nations, awards more power and authority to nations based on their economic, military, and historical circumstances than their demographic situation.

10. Only the United States, Russia, China, France, and England have veto powers that can overturn the majority opinion of other nation.

> 10. Is apathy just as harmful to humans as causing physical pain?

I disagree that apathy is just as harmful to humans as causing physical pain. Unjust and unwarranted anger and hatred is much more damaging to the human soul than apathy. The apathetic man may be persuaded to take up the challenge if given solid reasons for doing so. Indifference, however, is not an end, but merely a stage in the intellectual process.

As an example, take the inhumane events of the Holocaust in the 1940's. Americans were indifferent to the plight of the Jews throughout most of the war, hearing stories of persecution, but, since they had been subjected to dubious propaganda during the First World War, they were much more skeptical of anti-German propaganda during the early years of the second one.

The plight of the Jews was unknown until the liberation of the Kaufering camp in 1945. Indifference was washed away by righteous anger that led directly to the prosecution and in some cases execution of those responsible through the Nuremberg trials.

What led to the persecution of the Jews in the first pl

ace? Hatred, inculcated and long developed hatred and anger. I would say additionally that what held the Germans from doing anything while their brothers and sisters were subjected to their torments was not indifference but cowardice.

I do believe there is a causative relationship between indifference and the mass effect of genocide. The indifference of the German public to the Jewish plight under the Nazi regime was as detrimental as explicit support. Despite Nazi Germany being a single state totalitarian government, there was no significant domestic resistance against their governmental policies. Instead the German public was generally supportive of their government.

To sum up, although apathy to violence and prejudice does not prevent mass suffering, it is hardly the most significant factor to it. The major factor leading to suffering akin to the Holocaust is pure hatred against a minority group such as the German Jews.

## Model Sentences of Essay # 10

1. Unjust and unwarranted anger and hatred is much more damaging to the human soul than indifference.

2. Unjust and unwarranted anger and hatred is much more damaging to the human soul than apathy.

3. The apathetic man may be persuaded to take up the

challenge if given solid reasons for doing so.

4. Indifference, however, is not an end, but merely a stage in the intellectual process.

5. As an example, take the inhumane events of the Holocaust in the 1940's.

6. Americans were indifferent to the plight of the Jews throughout most of the war, hearing stories of persecution.

7. Since they had been subjected to dubious propaganda during the First World War, they were much more skeptical of anti-German propaganda.

8. The plight of the Jews was unknown until the liberation of the Kaufering camp in 1945.

9. Indifference was washed away by righteous anger that led directly to the prosecution and in some cases execution of those responsible through the Nuremberg trials.

10. What led to the persecution of the Jews in the first place?

11. Hatred, inculcated and long developed hatred and anger.

12. What held the Germans from doing anything while their brothers and sisters were subjected to their torments was not indifference but cowardice.

13. I do believe there is a causative relationship between indifference and the mass effect of genocide.

14. The indifference of the German public to the Jewish plight under the Nazi regime was as detrimental as explicit

support.

15. Despite Nazi Germany being a single state totalitarian government, there was no significant domestic resistance against their governmental policies.

16. Instead the German public was generally supportive of their government.

17. Although apathy to violence and prejudice does not prevent mass suffering, it is hardly the most significant factor to it.

18. The major factor leading to suffering akin to the Holocaust is pure hatred against a minority group such as the German Jews.

11. Is striving to achieve a goal always the best course of action, or should people give up if they are not making progress?

Imagine a world without the light bulb, without civil rights, or without the personal computer. If the forerunners of all of these concepts and inventions had given up at the first sign of failure then we would be living in a very different world today. Striving to achieve a goal is always the best course of action, even if it may seem like one is not making progress. Edison failed thousands of times before he finally progressed beyond failure and invented a working light bulb. Martin Luther King Jr. kept the fight for civil rights in America going, despite slow to no progress in the desegregation of America. Bill Gates stood stuck in the same place for years until finally moving forward to invent the personal computer.

Thomas Edison is known today as a great inventor, but this was not always the case. He was also known as the man who just couldn't get it right, when it came to certain inventions. He made no progress for years in the area of electricity and if had given up, who is to know how long we would have lived with oil lanterns and candlelight lamps. D espite failing again, and again, Edison forged ahead, becoming one of the most important inventors in history. The light bulb hasn't changed much from what Edison designed years ago, but it was only possible because he worked toward achieving his goals.

Progress in the desegregation movement in America was slow moving if not completely sedentary during the time of the great Rev. Martin Luther King Jr. Despite great opposition from the majority white population in the South and government officials, King moved forward striving towards the equality he so desperately want for himself and the other African Americans in the United States. His tenacity inspired others to join the fight, creating a movement. It all culminated into his moving "I have a dream speech" which is still used to inspire people around the world. If Martin Luther has given up at the first sign of no progress, we might be living in a very different America. Instead we have an African-American President and separate and equal is no longer an accepted practice.

Bill Gates dropped out of school, only to become one of the richest men in America. It took him several years to develop the PC and Windows operating system. He has single handily changed the face of communication in today's s ociety. Had he stopped at the first sign on difficulty, we might not have the technology we have today.

Progress doesn't always come quickly, and sometimes it doesn't come at all. What separates ordinary people from extraordinary people and their ground breaking inventions and influence, is tenacity. From Thomas Edison to Rev. Martin Luther King Jr., and Bill Gates, the point that striving to achieve ones goals is more important than quitting is resoundingly clear.

## Model Sentences of Essay # 11

1. If the forerunners of all of these concepts and inventions had given up at the first sign of failure then we would be living in a very different world today.

2. Edison failed thousands of times before he finally progressed beyond failure and invented a working light bulb.

3. Progress in the desegregation movement in America was slow moving if not completely sedentary during the time of the great Rev. Martin Luther King Jr.

4. Despite great opposition from the majority white population in the South and government officials, King moved forward striving towards the equality he so desperately want for himself and African Americans in the United States.

5. Despite failing again, and again, Edison forged ahead,

becoming one of the most important inventors in history.

6. It all culminated into his moving "I have a dream speech" which is still used to inspire people around the world.

7. Bill Gates stood stuck in the same place for years until finally moving forward to invent the personal computer.

8. Progress in the desegregation movement in America was slow moving if not completely sedentary during the time of the great Rev. Martin Luther King Jr.

9. It all culminated into his moving "I have a dream speech" which is still used to inspire people around the world.

What separates ordinary people from extraordinary people and their ground breaking inventions and influence, is tenacity.

> 12. Are people more efficient when confronted with the expectations and demands of others?

In this post-modern society nobody is free from the demands or expectations of others, whether one is a toddler and expected to walk by a certain age or a father expected to provide a comfortable life for his family. People are bound by the demands and expectations of others in every culture throughout the world, however the demands set forth for an individual do not necessarily further productivity. The expectations or demands of an individual lead to increased productivity only if one aims for a desired outcome and is willing to put forth the additional effort.

Productivity differs from one individual to another and depends on the setting in which one defines productivity. High school students are the epitome of subjective productivity. The goal and expectation of students once they graduate from high school, which is well accepted in society, is to attend a college or university. Although, most students tend to graduate from local or state universities, there are only a select few who manage to get accepted to elite schools. Each student decides, consciously or subconsciously, what is important and what one wants. As a result, the studen ts themselves, in the end, are responsible for their education. So, a student must have the passion and desire to attain an elite education, and must meet and, in most cases, surpass demands and expectations.

Despite a strong desire for a specific outcome, one must be willing to set out and put forth the effort. Many people want to attend and reap the privileges of attending an elite university, however desire will only get one so far. Many people also dream of living an elegant and extravagant lifestyle, but few actually do what is necessary to attain such a dream. Desire to work through the hardships and challenges that coincide with working towards a goal is the most important characteristic one must possess.

Demands and expectations are inescapable, but the level of productivity one yields depends on the desire for a goal and willingness to work. As delved into above, a student must desire academic success and be willing to put forth the effort to attain the goal. If both are met, then comes increased productivity which, in high school, means top-notch grades and other extra-curricular activities. Although, this simplifies the requirements for increasing productivity for a student, one must keep in mind that each setting differs, but one must have the desire and willingness to work.

<u>Model Sentences of Essay # 12</u>

1. People are bound by the demands and expectations of others in every culture throughout the world, however the demands set forth for an individual does not necessarily further productivity.

2. The expectations or demands of an individual leads to increased productivity only if one aims for a desired outcome and is willing to put forth the additional effort.

3. So, a student must have the passion and desire to attain an elite education, and must meet and, in most cases, surpass demands and expectations.

4. Many people want to attend and reap the privileges of attending an elite university, however desire will only get one so far.

5. As delved into above, a student must desire academic success and be willing to put forth the effort to attain the goal.

6. Demands and expectations are inescapable, but the level of productivity one yields depends on the desire for a goal and willingness to work.

Although, this simplifies the requirements for increasing productivity for a student, one must keep in mind that each setting differs.

## 13. Should people quit pursuing their goals when all hope is lost?

Without passion, optimism and the willingness to believe in the past, many accomplishments in this world, including the light bulb, might never have come to fruition. At the same time, many lives have been wasted chasing the rainbow's end. Similar to what my grandmother used to say, "Everything in moderation, including moderation," it is important that decisions are formulated and followed according to a delicate balance.

Tim LaHaye, in his book on personality and temperament, theorizes that what makes a great business owner or salesperson is an indomitable spirit. It is said that, to be an effective entrepreneur, one must devote 16 hours of his day towards the business, with the remaining eight hours for sleeping. Many people would quit pursuing their goal if sixteen hours of their waking life is needed to accomplish it. And the need to persevere is not limited by any means to business. Where would Helen Keller have wound up if Anne Sullivan had decided that she was a hopeless case? Knowing if and when to give up on something can change the cou rse and tenor of one's entire life.

On the flip side, similar to my grandmother's advice, my experience working as a paralegal at a bankruptcy firm, has taught me that many people hold on too long - pursuing a dream until it devours them not only financially, but emotionally and socially as well. Not giving up often has costs we are unwilling to pay. The famous dancer Teri Garr was known for her beautiful legs, but after being diagnosed with multiple sclerosis her doctor gave her the choice to give up skirts for braces and pants or give up walking. There are times in life that present itself with only the option to quit, forcing us to grudgingly move towards a new direction.

Janice Kaihoi, nurse and mother of two, decided not to fight when diagnosed with a rare and almost incurable form of cancer. She chose to embrace the remainder of her life with her family and live it to the fullest rather than put herself (and her family) through months of tension and sickness from experimental treatments. Many people around the world face equally difficult decisions when deciding whether to stay with abusive or negligent spouses in order to keep their families together. The decision to call it quits can be an excruciating one, but at times letting go can be the best thing for everyone involved.

Like anything else in life, it's a question of balance. Some choices are easier to make than others. Whether to continue casually learning guitar, for example, somehow feels less weighty than whether or not to pursue a career in counseling. It is not truly (for most) a question of giving up or continued pursuit, but a question of what to pursue. Perhaps giving up is just an indication that whatever was is not as important as what we sacrificed it to. If something is a real passion, the odds are it will resurface again in another way even if the first course you took didn't work out.

## Model Sentences of Essay # 13

1. Without passion, optimism and the willingness to believe in the past, many accomplishments in this world, including the light bulb, might never have come to fruition.

2. Similar to what my grandmother used to say, "Everything in moderation, including moderation," it is important that decisions are formulated and followed according to a delicate balance.

3. It is said that, to be an effective entrepreneur, one must devote 16 hours of their day towards the business, with the remaining eight hours for sleeping.

4. Where would Helen Keller have wound up if Anne

Sullivan had decided that she was a hopeless case?

5. On the flip side, similar to my grandmother's advice, my experience working as a paralegal at a bankruptcy firm has taught me that many people hold on too long - pursuing a dream until it devours them not only financially, but also emotionally and socially.

6. There are times in life that present itself with only the option to quit, forcing us to grudgingly move towards a new direction.

7. She chose to embrace the remainder of her life with her family and live it to the fullest rather than put herself (and her family) through months of tension and sickness from experimental treatments.

8. Many people around the world face equally difficult decisions when deciding whether to stay with abusive or negligent spouses in order to keep their families together.

9. The decision to call it quits can be an excruciating one, but at times letting go can be the best thing for everyone involved.

10. If something is a real passion, the odds are it will resurface again in another way even if the first course you took didn't work out.

## 14. Where do values and beliefs held by society come from?

Established values in a society originate from many sources, such as the culture, religions, and values and beliefs that a society or country was founded upon. In any given society the values of each individual vary from person to person. But there are, of course, well-accepted values throughout any society, and these values are historically present in the popular culture of a society. Whether it's the entertainment industry or health sector, the values are ingrained in the pop-culture of a society. However, there are always outliers that attempt to promote behavior or ideals that are not consistent with the values of a society.

In a society where pop-culture is synonymous with entertainment, such as the United States, it might be difficult to recognize any form of values that Americans treasure from a superficial glimpse of America. Yet, from the archetypal stories and hearsay heard at every social venue, American values are embodied. Classic stories, such as Batman, display the timeless value very dear to Americans: good over evil. From the very beginning of the idea of America, the citizens have always believed that good should prevail in an y situation. This value is very apparent today and is displayed in every aspect of the culture, from politics to advertising. At social gatherings people constantly discusses the changes in one's family and future prospects.

Despite the conspicuous values of Americans, there are few who exploit how fast information is disseminated and the shock value of such information. The popularity of such questionable and shocking trends is difficult to comprehend. Such an example is Paris Hilton. What culture which strongly believes in freedom, good over evil, and charity holds such a character as Paris Hilton to her level of popularity? The answer might not be simple, however when one examines the typical "Paris fan", it becomes simple enough. It is obvious that only a very small percentage of the roughly 300 million Americans believe that having adult footage publically available is a good thing. Trends and fads are not permanent, and it is the temporary following of the few who seem to dominate the pop-culture scene.

Values and beliefs that are held by the citizens of nations and the society within them are derived from a multitude of sources. With the case of America, television programming and music give birth to, and are reflections of, the culture of the country. The values of a society are not alwa ys apparent at first, however if one becomes familiar with a particular culture, then the values are mostly reflected in the pop-culture of the examined society.

## Model Sentences of Essay # 14

1. Established values in a society originate from many sources, such as the culture, religions, and values and beliefs that a society or country was founded upon.

2. Whether it's the entertainment industry or health sector, the values are ingrained in the pop-culture of a society.

3. In a society where pop-culture is synonymous with entertainment, such as the United States, it might be difficult to recognize any form of values that Americans treasure from a superficial glimpse of America.

4. Classic stories, such as Batman, display the timeless value very dear to Americans: good over evil.

5. Trends and fads are not permanent, and it is the temporary following of the few who seem to dominate the pop-culture scene.

6. Values and beliefs that are held by the citizens of nations and the society within them are derived from a multitude of sources.

7. With the case of America, television programming and music give birth to, and are reflections of, the culture of the country.

8. The values of a society are not always apparent at first,

however if one becomes familiar with a particular culture, then the values are mostly reflected in the pop-culture of the examined society.

9. Despite the conspicuous values of Americans, there are few who exploit how fast information is disseminated and the shock value of such information.

10. What culture which strongly believes in freedom, good over evil, and charity holds such a character as Paris Hilton to her level of popularity?

> 15. Are conquered dreams and aspirations of people the definition of success?

Consider, if you will, the Roman empire. Quests to conquer the world are full of what Sheri Zampelli would term, "greatest wishes and ambitions." But that does not necessarily mean that they benefit society. It depends on who is doing the conquering. Louisa May Alcott wrote in her short story "A Modern Mephistopheles," about a man who manipulated another into financial success only to observe his moral and psychological decay. More innocent but much more personal and prevalent are parents who, pursuing their dreams and goals of having successful children, push those children into long hours of study or careers they don't enjoy. Sometimes the realization of one person's goals can cost another theirs.

Who are the people pursuing their inner desires and have bettered society? Amy Carmichael spent her life caring for orphaned and abandoned children in India during the late 1800's, saving hundreds of young girls from becoming shrine prostitutes. Bill Gates founded a computer empire that jettisoned us into the modern age. Jean Valjean, of literary and operatic fame, escaped from prison and spent the remainder of his life making a fortune and helping the poor and needy. Their goals were widely different, but they each started out to improve the lives of those around them.

Perhaps what is most concerning in modern day descriptions of success is that people try to frame it as unselfish - as something deserved. Few, if any, goals are unselfish. Even the desire to be self-sacrificing is often a selfish one, enabling us to feel a superiority towards others. Whether or not society as a whole benefits from our desires or ambition depends entirely on what we set out to accomplish, however, I would have to agree with Ms. Zampelli that the world would be better off if people felt less guilty, or at least less sorry for themselves, for doing what they want.

Model Sentences of Essay # 15

1. Quests to conquer the world are full of what Sheri Zampelli would term, "greatest wishes and ambitions."

2. Louisa May Alcott wrote in her short story "A Modern Mephistopheles," about a man who manipulated another into financial success only to observe his moral and psychological decay.

3. More innocent but much more personal and prevalent are parents who, pursuing their dreams and goals of having successful children, push those children into long hours of study or careers they don't enjoy.

4. Amy Carmichael spent her life caring for orphaned and

abandoned children in India during the late 1800's, saving hundreds of young girls from becoming shrine prostitutes.

5. Bill Gates founded a computer empire that jettisoned us into the modern age.

6. Jean Val jean, of literary and operatic fame, escaped from prison and spent the remainder of his life making a fortune and helping the poor and needy.

7. Even the desire to be self-sacrificing is often a selfish one, enabling us to feel a superiority towards others.

8. Whether or not society as a whole benefits from our desires or ambition depends entirely on what we set out to accomplish, however, I would have to agree with Ms. Zampelli that the world would be better off if people felt less guilty, or at least less sorry for themselves, for doing what they want.

16. Does the media provide an accurate analysis of the events of today?

Many people think the media sensationalize the news. It portrays images and stories in a way to evoke the maximum amount of human emotion. I think the media does focus on negative news more than positive news, but I don't see a problem with it. Media outlets have become separate industries that run on profit. The best way to make profit is through advertising, and advertisers only want to place ads in magazines, newspapers, and on TV news shows that sell or are popular. The reality is that people don't want to read about the latest charity work someone did, they want to read about the triple homicide that occurred in their city. Violence, and sensationalized news sells, it's what people want to read, and watch. It is also perhaps a reflection of the world's true nature.

I, like many others, like to read about events and stories that are different from my own life. Stories about crime, and war catch my attention, while feel-good ,fluff stories do not. The news sometimes exaggerates events creating an almost movie like experience for the consumer. Real life is always more interesting than fiction, which is why people watch the news. The media outlets are only giving people what they want to watch. If anyone is to blame for the amount of negative news stories we read and watch, it is us, the viewers.

Some people try to argue that things are not as bad as the media portrays them. This is especially true when it comes to news footage and stories concerning the war and the crime rate of various locations. The truth may be that things are actually a lot worse than what the media portrays. War, for example, is full of casualties, blood, gore, and sheer violence. The media probably only portrays a fraction of the atrocities that occur during war. If anything, media makes far away concepts real in our everyday life.

I don't think the media focuses too much on the bad in the world. I think they report on what people want to watch and what sells. Also, many of their stories are actually not as bad as what is happening in reality, and are many times accurate. However, no matter how you feel on topic, your choices are limited, as most of all media outlets in in the world are owned by just a handful of agencies that control what you see and read.

## Model Sentences of Essay # 16

1. The best way to make profit is through advertising, and advertisers only want to place ads in magazines, newspapers, and on TV news shows that sell or are popular.

2. Violence, and sensationalized news sells, it's what people want to read, and watch.

3. Some people try to argue that things are not as bad as the media portrays them.

4. War, for example, is full of causalities, blood, gore, and sheer violence.

5. This is especially true when it comes to news footage and stories concerning the war and the crime rate of various locations.

6. Many of their stories are actually not as bad as what is happening in reality, and are many times accurate.

7. However, no matter how you feel on a topic, your choices are limited, as most of all media outlets in the world are owned by just a handful of agencies that control what you see and read.

> 17. Is it better to rush sometimes and take action, or is it better to take time and investigate first?

The Apollo astronauts are no doubt pioneers in manned space flight to the moon. At the time, they risked not only their lives, but also their national reputation and pride. The countless man-hours and personnel that contributed to the new NASA space program were not in vain. The preparation involved was titanic, not because astronauts were afraid to perish, but because the consequences of failure in reaching the goal set by the late President Kennedy were worse: losing the "space race" to the Soviets. The amount of preparation needed for any problem or challenge is never the same, and should never be more than required for the situation at hand. Learning as much as possible before acting in most situations is not necessary, unlike the Apollo Space Program, because the outcome is easily anticipated and excessive preparation is a waste of resources. Thus, people should learn as much as possible for situations that will result in increased benefits or failure that results in irreplaceable losses.

Most people agree that the amount of preparation is proportional to the rate of success in any given situation.

However, the extent of taking action and preparation vary considerably, such as studying for an exam and learning to fly a plane for the first time. The amount of learning and studying before taking action should reflect the desire for the most favorable outcome. One may not truly learn everything about flying a plane from a book, but if the amount of preparation taken is very high then it can increase the likelihood of the desired outcome: survival. Surely one would not prepare equally as much before playing a video game as one does for preparing for actual manned flight. Nevertheless, the individual is responsible for the amount of learning that should take place before taking an action.

Learning as much as possible before doing anything seems like the best way to approach an unfamiliar situation, however it is not necessary in most situations. According to Wang Yang-ming, from *A Source Book in Chinese Philosophy*, there are people who prefer to learn as much as possible for a situation before putting their knowledge into practice. This is not an efficient method to approach problems or put certain skills into use. One may learn quite a bit of theory from a book, but the real education comes from actually practicing a skill or carrying out an action. One may choose to learn as much as possible to ascertain the sense and ex perience of flying on a plane, but this type of preparation is not applicable. Also, knowing how to swim is another example of how one cannot adequately prepare until one has gotten into a pool.

Learning a new skill, making a decision or solving a problem all requires a certain level of preparation. The amount of preparation and learning should fully reflect the translation between learning and taking action. In this way, precious resources, such as time, money and possibly lives, are not squandered. One should always remember, however, that although one may seem more than prepared before acting, experience is something that can never be learned from a book. In other words, experience serves information, and one can only begin reaping the benefits of valuable information through trial and error.

## Model Sentences of Essay # 17

1. The preparation involved was titanic, not because astronauts were afraid to perish, but because the consequences of failure in reaching the goal set by the late President Kennedy were worse: losing the "space race" to the Soviets.

2. However, the extent of taking action and preparation vary considerably, such as studying for an exam and learning to fly a plane for the first time.

3. One may not truly learn everything about flying a plane from a book, but if the amount of preparation taken is very high then it can increase the likelihood of the desired outcome: survival.

4. Learning as much as possible before doing anything seems like the best way to approach an unfamiliar situation, however it is not necessary in most situations.

5. Surely one would not prepare equally as much before playing a video game as one does for preparing for actual manned flight.

6. The amount of preparation and learning should fully reflect the translation between learning and taking action.

7. In this way, precious resources, such as time, money and possibly lives, are not squandered.

8. In other words, experience serves information, and one can only begin reaping the benefits of valuable information through trial and error.

## 18. Should humor be the preferred route for approaching difficult situations and problems?

There is no doubt that problems plague humanity in every crevasse of life ranging in magnitude as diverse as people themselves. Just as so, there are also many ways to solve or alleviate life's problems. Despite the limitless entirety of potential solutions most are inappropriate and excessive. One such coping technique that can putatively be applied to difficult situations is humor. Laughter is a naturally occurring pleasant phenomenon, but the contemporary recommended usage of it could result in unwanted consequences. Although some difficulties may require additional resources in terms of problem solving, time, or other means, certain problems concerning the well-being and mental health of people should not be approached lightly. Thus, I believe that using humor is not the best way to approach difficult situations.

According to Marshall Brain, the author of *How Laughter Works*, people are actually being taught to laugh at situations and things that are not necessarily humorous to cope with difficult situations. This technique may seem like a positive method to handle stressful and unpleasant situations.

However, it can potentially cause more harm than good. If one is taught to use humor to bear a situation, this may in turn result in a diminished value and importance placed upon said situation. Just as in Pavlov's famous conditioning psychology experiments, where a physiological response was induced from a deliberate external stimulus over a period of time. The same can occur when using humor in the recommended manner. This is, however, an extreme case of what could happen. Nevertheless, the conditioning of the mind in any case can result in unforeseen consequences. One may teach themselves to laugh at friends getting hurt, and in the future the person may find it difficult to take other situations seriously, and may also in turn result in social rejection to some degree.

One should not attempt to ease any degree of mental anxiety or stress using one approach, no matter how mild. This would be akin to treating a cancer patient with only one procedure. However, I do believe that it should be used as a supplement to a more rigorous solution or treatment. The best way to approach difficult situations is being methodical and logical. Humor should be used to lessen the degree of a given situation or perhaps as a closure aid when a situation has been overcome, not the first or only approac

h. In cases of chronic situations, humor should definitely be integrated to aid in the recovery process of such situations as depression. This is consistent with current mental health care recommendations from any psychologist. There is a time and place for everything, and humor is no exception. Humor should be used as a supplement in coping with a difficult situation.

Humor is an excellent tool to distract one from the pains of reality. It also has the amazing ability to reduce the severity of a situation. When used in the appropriate contexts, humor is an excellent tool. However, it should never be used as the primary method to cope with a difficult situation. In any case, humor may seem ideal, but too much of a good thing will almost always result in more maladies.

## Model Sentences of Essay # 18

1. There is no doubt that problems plague humanity in every crevasse of life ranging in magnitude as diverse as people themselves.

2. One such coping technique that can putatively be applied to difficult situations is humor.

3. Although some difficulties may require additional resources in terms of problem solving, time, or other means, certain problems concerning the well-being and mental health of people should not be approached lightly.

4. If one is taught to use humor to bear a situation, this may in turn result in a diminished value and importance placed upon said situation.

5. Just as in Pavlov's famous conditioning psychology experiments, where a physiological response was induced from a deliberate external stimulus over a period of time.

6. One should not attempt to ease any degree of mental anxiety or stress using one approach, no matter how mild.

7. Humor should be used to lessen the degree of a given situation or perhaps as a closure aid when a situation has been overcome, not the first or only approach.

8. Humor should be used as a supplement in coping with a difficult situation.

9. In any case, humor may seem ideal, but too much of a good thing will almost always result in more maladies.

10. However, I do believe that it should be used as a supplement to a more rigorous solution or treatment.

> 19. Are all people dependent on a social network and family, even if they choose a life of solitude?

Hilary Clinton quoted a West African proverb that said, "It takes a village to raise a family." The idea behind this simple line is complex. It implies that children need a support system, a community or a family to thrive in life and make it to adulthood and beyond. I think everyone needs a family, network or community in life, and that this idea is reflected all around the world taking many different forms. Family, or community provide support, wisdom and guidance. The need to belong is universal.

In West Africa tribal communities live together as large units. Here family takes the form of communal establishments where everyone plays a part in raising children, and household tasks. In Africa such family is necessary, as lonely individuals, or even single units of families would be unable to complete all the tasks needed to survive in the harsh environment. The building of communal families was instrumental for the survival of various African tribal communities.

In countries where one can survive alone, like the U.S, the family remains an important aspect of society. Even with a divorce rate of 50%, Americans remain dedicated to the idea of family and community. It is now simply taking a different form. The "modern American family" is usually blended, consisting of step fathers, mothers, and step siblings. Despite marriages not surviving in the U.S., the idea of family is thriving. Nowhere is the idea that everyone needs a family or family like unit more prevalent than in the prison system. In prison, even criminals come together to form gangs, and makeshift families, so that they feel like they belong. Another example of the importance of family is reflected in suicide rates. Most people who commit suicide feel "alone" and usually don't feel as if they belong anywhere.

For humans, the need for contact and connection is important. People in all countries, and situations seek out companionship. Having a family has become a basic human need, like shelter or food.

## Model Sentences of Essay # 19

1. It implies that children need a support system, a community or a family to thrive in life and make it to adulthood and beyond.

2. Here family takes the form of communal establishments where everyone plays a part in raising children, and household tasks.

3. Even with a divorce rate of 50%, Americans remain dedicated to the idea of family and community.

4. The "modern American family" is usually blended, consisting of step fathers, mothers, and step siblings.

5. In prison, even criminals come together to form gangs, and makeshift families, so that they feel like they belong.

6. People in all countries, and situations seek out companionship.

7. Having a family has become a basic human need, like shelter or food.

> 20. Do you agree that our society has become too negative and less sensitive?

Looking at the condition of modern society begs the question: have we become overly cynical and desensitized? Ironically, we must also ask if there is hope to end this culture of cynicism. It is clear that it is time for a change, but it will be difficult because cynicism is so deeply entrenched in our perceptions of the world. According to Positive Psychologist Mihaly Csikszentmihalyi, much of modern "human development", including humanities, politics, science and technology has ignored basic human strengths and virtues that are worth cultivating. The leadership in both academia and "the real world" has been taken over by those who have promoted this culture of self-congratulatory cynicism. This trend has overflowed from the "ivory tower" of the elite into everyday lives of everyday people.

According to a recent political survey in the United States, the common citizen believes that the next ten years will not be as good as the last. People no longer seem to see the joy in the little things that make life worth living. This trend seems especially apparent in young people who are being force-fed a commercialized vision of "the good life" an d at the same moment, are bombarded with violence, melodramatic babble, and expansive wealth. These extremes desensitize the viewer to such an extent that many now are unable to value basic human experiences.

This culture of cynicism stems from the basic fact that people have lost faith in "progress." The advances in science, technology, art and philosophy, which are meant to bring people forward, has not prevented world wars, depression, poverty and sickness. If anything, this "progress" has pulled us further away from what is truly important, people. In order to turn our society around and bring us back to "our roots" if you will, it is necessary to change our perception of "progress."

Progress must start positive cultural values. Each individual must recognize the importance of long-term happiness; that what pleases us in the moment won't necessarily make us happy later in life, and we must recognize those that rejoice in the simple fact of being human. Once this new definition of progress is adopted and joined with "traditional" progress, the general perception of the future will change. People will no longer believe that we are headed down a doomed path. We will naturally make choices that take into account the well-being of everyone and this culture of c ynicism will develop into a culture of optimism.

## Model Sentences of Essay # 20

1. Looking at the condition of modern society begs the question: have we become overly cynical and desensitized?

2. According to Positive Psychologist Mihaly Csikszentmihalyi, much of modern "human development", including humanities, politics, science and technology has ignored basic human strengths and virtues that are worth cultivating.

3. The leadership in both academia and "the real world" has been taken over by those who have promoted this culture of self-congratulatory cynicism.

4. This trend seems especially apparent in young people who are being force-fed a commercialized vision of "the good life" and at the same moment, are bombarded with violence, melodramatic babble, and expansive wealth.

5. These extremes desensitize the viewer to such an extent that many now are unable to value basic human experiences.

6. The advances in science, technology, art and philosophy, which are meant to bring people forward, have not prevented world wars, depression, poverty and sickness.

7. In order to turn our society around and bring us back to "our roots" if you will, it is necessary to change our perception of "progress."

> 21. Do you believe art and creativity should always be associated with anguish, suffering, and pain?

Nowadays, creativity manifests itself in seemingly endless forms throughout all fields of study. Every field from complex quantum mechanics to modern dance, creative individuals have undertaken novel, often unsuccessful, paths in their careers. Without these pioneering people, fields in art and science would lay stagnant. Although great strides have been made in art and science, the 'artists' have been the ones that have endured criticism, from others, and seemingly worse, themselves. Artists are constantly pursuing perfection, and it seems that the best nurturers for their creativity are themselves. Although tending to creativity and striving for perfection are important, they can also lead to destructive behaviors.

Many well-known and unfamiliar artists have succumbed to misery in one form or another. Whether suffering unfolds in episodes of depression or chemical dependency, the reason is almost always related to creative roadblocks. Fortunately, most roadblocks are short-lived and rarely develop into serious afflictions. However, in some cases, misery is a common component among artists before they ever st art creating artistic works. Art may become one's escape from reality or melancholy that may have served as motivation. In the case of J. K. Rowling, she endured years of hardship and secretly wrote about a young boy who would become a famous wizard to escape her reality. Many famous artists throughout time have become famous because of their works, rather than their episodes of grief.

In conclusion, the pattern of grief about one's work seems to be more prevalent these days. This awareness is perhaps due to advancements in communication and the subsequent "shrinking" of the world. Artistry, as a result, has been labeled a field with inescapable heartache. There are thousands of artists throughout the world, and the association of anguish with creativity is the consequence of a minute group of audacious artists. In every society, there are few people who crave attention in any form, positive or negative. Perhaps if these few people cannot be successful in their endeavors in creativity, they dwell in the spotlight of torment.

Like many professions, artists experience anguish. The experiences of artists in grief are almost always short-lived. Anguish is not a permanent disposition, but serves as a creative hurdle, one that must be overcome in order to flour ish. The stereotype that artists will ultimately be miserable is false; it is thought so by the few ill-natured people that depict this grim lifestyle. It is the responsibility of art enthusiasts to realize that anguish is not exclusive to artists.

## Model Sentences of Essay # 21

1. Nowadays, creativity manifests itself in seemingly endless forms throughout all fields of study.

2. Every field from complex quantum mechanics to modern dance, creative individuals have undertaken novel, often unsuccessful, paths in their careers

3. Artists are constantly pursuing perfection, and it seems that the best nurturers for their creativity are themselves.

4. Whether suffering unfolds in episodes of depression or chemical dependency, the reason is almost always related to creative roadblocks.

5. Art may become one's escape from reality or melancholy that may have served as motivation.

6. Artistry, as a result, has been labeled a field with inescapable heartache.

7. Perhaps if these few people cannot be successful in their endeavors in creativity, they dwell in the spotlight of torment.

8. Anguish is not a permanent disposition, but serves as a creative hurdle, one that must be overcome in order to flourish.

9. There are thousands of artists throughout the world, and the association of anguish with creativity is the consequence of a minute group of audacious artists.

10. Although tending to creativity and striving for perfection are important, they can also lead to destructive behaviors.

> 22. Is life predetermined or do people have the ability to pave their own paths in life?

The search for answers to all life's mysteries is an inherent part of the human psyche. Throughout history, human beings have invented numerous theories to explain paranormal and metaphysical phenomenon. Before important discoveries, such as microscopic organisms and their role in diseases, many believed that certain malicious behaviors caused such disease, and a "higher power" was ultimately responsible for their fate. The notion that our lives are premeditated, whether by a higher being or not, is nonsense.

In W. W. Jacob's *The Monkey's Paw*, a supposed enchanted talisman held the power to grant three wishes to three men. Each wish would be granted, however, the wish would not be granted in a fairy-tale manner, but in a seemingly coincidental way. In the story, the father wished for a sum of money and he was granted his wish, but was granted it in an unforeseen trade for his son's life. In a scene prior to the son's death and payment of the money, the family is gathered and the father wishes for a sum of money. Afterwards, the son says, "Well, I don't see the money, and I bet I never shall." Although this story shows that wishing is magi cal and coincidental, the son himself is most likely responsible for the outcome. Perhaps feeling that the family greatly desired the money, the son took matters into his own hands.

The idea that each of our lives is predetermined is not logical. People make hundreds, if not thousands, of decisions a day. The sheer complexity of human beings' thought processes consequently results in inconsistent decision-making. Add countless daily influences to this already dynamic high functioning being, and the notion of destiny is absurd. Coincidences and events that one believes lead to destiny are merely a result of including people in one's life; whether they share similar beliefs or are integral in lifestyle or career.

Destiny is a human invention designed to explain seemingly impossible coincidences and fantastic events. Though destiny may appear to be paranormal or the responsibility of a higher power, it is perhaps an unborn precursor to a novel science in sociology or other related field. The choices one makes can directly or indirectly affect another individual, however, the magnitude of the affect depends on the choice itself. Therefore, one's 'destiny' is not predetermined; rather it is the responsibility of each individual to sculpt his or her own life.

## Model Sentences of Essay # 22

1. The search for answers to all life's mysteries is an inherent part of the human psyche.

2. Throughout history, human beings have invented numerous theories to explain paranormal and metaphysical phenomenon.

3. Before important discoveries, such as microscopic organisms and their role in diseases, many believed that certain malicious behaviors caused such disease, and a "higher power" was ultimately responsible for their fate.

4. In the story, the father wished for a sum of money and he was granted his wish, but was granted it in an unforeseen trade for his son's life.

5. Perhaps feeling that the family greatly desired the money, the son took matters into his own hands.

6. The sheer complexity of human beings' thought processes consequently results in inconsistent decision-making.

7. Add countless daily influences to this already dynamic high functioning being, and the notion of destiny is absurd.

> 23. Should the definition of courage be restricted to people who risk their own well-being for the good of others or should it also be expanded to people who uphold values?

Courageous deeds fit into a variety of categories. Though acts of self-sacrifice for the sake of others are without a doubt courageous, we need not use such conservative nomenclature in discussing human behavior. One can argue semantics regarding the differences in connotation among words such as "adventuresome" and "courageous," but the decision to allow the word courage to have a broader range of meaning remains valid, and in some ways any attempt to do otherwise merely belittles the actions of courageous men and women.

One can see examples of courage in many endeavors other than unselfish acts of heroism. Was Rosa Parks not courageous in her unwillingness to be deemed a second-class citizen and sit at the back of the bus in Montgomery, Alabama? Were the men and women killed in Tiananmen Square while standing up to the PRC government not courageous? Equating these heroic actions with "....differ[ing] from the mainstream in one's preferences in fashion or music

" is simply insulting. Wearing leopard-print shoes is not courageous; standing up to a force greater than you in the name of justice is the definition of courage.

Cases need not be so extreme to warrant the usage of the word courageous. It takes true courage to do many deeds not nearly as lofty as those of Rosa Parks and others. Being true to oneself about what one really wants in life is an act of incredible courage. A genuine, unfeigned decision takes tremendous honesty and courage to make: honesty to be willing to say what you want, and courage to do so. Even things like bungee jumping and skydiving require a certain degree of courage. Again, there are indeed slight differences between words like "courage" and "daring", but they are futile and ultimately meaningless distinctions in regards to a discussion of people's actions.

Attempting to make certain acts seem more worthy than others by calling them courageous is not of value. In fact, to call these actions anything less than courageous is to disparage the efforts of men and women of the past and present who deserve a greater level of respect.

## Model Sentences of Essay # 23

1. One can argue semantics regarding the differences in connotation among words such as "adventuresome" and

"courageous," but the decision to allow the word courage to have a broader range of meaning remains valid, and in some ways any attempt to do otherwise merely belittles the actions of courageous men and women.

2. Equating these heroic actions with "....differ[ing] from the mainstream in one's preferences in fashion or music" is simply insulting.

3. Wearing leopard-print shoes is not courageous; standing up to a force greater than you in the name of justice is the definition of courage.

4. Cases need not be so extreme to warrant the usage of the word courageous.

5. A genuine, unfeigned decision takes tremendous honesty and courage to make: honesty to be willing to say what you want, and courage to do so.

6. Again, there are indeed slight differences between words like "courage" and "daring", but they are futile and ultimately meaningless distinctions in regards to a discussion of people's actions.

7. In fact, to call these actions anything less than courageous is to disparage the efforts of men and women of the past and present who deserve a greater level of respect.

## 24. Is it feasible for a society to simultaneously offer perfect equality and perfect freedom?

When Thomas Jefferson wrote into the constitution " ...all men are created equal", he did not intend to sound off as though he believed that all men have identical abilities, flaws, ambitions, and dreams. He meant that we are all equal in the eyes of God and the law. We can aspire to that kind of equality, but aspiring to even approach equality in other ways necessarily compromises the freedom of individuals.

Helping people with limited opportunities or abilities to have decent lives requires money. This money must come from people who have more; if the government does not have the money to help the poor, they will continue to suffer. If we believe that citizens should have the basics of life, such as food, shelter, and healthcare, thus making them to a degree more equal with more prosperous people, one of the freedoms of the rich, the freedom to do whatever they want with their money, must be compromised. We end up with neither perfect equality nor perfect freedom, but someplace in between, where everyone has something.

Anatole France wrote sarcastically, "The law, in its ma

jestic equality, forbids the rich as well as the poor to beg in the streets, steal bread, or sleep under a bridge." We are, in principle if not fully in reality, both free and equal under the law. In the real world, however, some people, through education, innate ability, family connections, or money, have far more opportunities than others; they eat better, travel more freely, enjoy life more, and live longer. That's fine; true communism leads only to misery, because human nature demands more for the self and less for strangers. But we can at least attempt to give the poorest among us a meal, a bed, and a chance.

In the end, we can't be both truly free and truly equal. There is a balance that must be held, with perfect equality and perfect freedom being constantly undergoing a negotiation. The fact is that these two wonderful ideals are always, to a degree, at war, and the only way to lasting justice lies in reaching a peace treaty between the two. We must respect both.

## Model Sentences of Essay # 24

1. When Thomas Jefferson wrote into the constitution "...all men are created equal", he did not intend to sound off as though he believed that all men have identical abilities, flaws, ambitions, and dreams.

2. We can aspire to that kind of equality, but aspiring to even approach equality in other ways necessarily compromises the freedom of individuals.

3. Anatole France wrote sarcastically, "The law, in its majestic equality, forbids the rich as well as the poor to beg in the streets, steal bread, or sleep under a bridge."

4. We are, in principle if not fully in reality, both free and equal under the law.

5. In the real world, however, some people, through education, innate ability, family connections, or money, have far more opportunities than others; they eat better, travel more freely, enjoy life more, and live longer.

6. There is a balance that must be held, with perfect equality and perfect freedom being constantly undergoing a negotiation.

7. The fact is that these two wonderful ideals are always, to a degree, at war, and the only way to lasting justice lies in reaching a peace treaty between the two.

> 25. Are there social situations when impolite behavior is necessary?

Good manners have virtually disappeared from our self-centered world. People butt into line at the supermarket, guests on political news shows shout at each other, fist fights break out in the Korean National Assembly. Many believe that it's essential to be rude or aggressive to change the world for the better. Of course, each person thinks that his version of "better" is the only one that counts, and that leads to anger on all sides. Actually, though, it is better to be as polite as possible in all circumstances, even when that is not the same as never offending anyone.

The twentieth century's greatest moral leaders, the people who truly improved the world, conducted themselves with great dignity and politeness. Mahatma Gandhi, Nelson Mandela, and Martin Luther King, Jr. achieved great things by loving their enemies while calmly and politely demonstrating against their moral failures. The great religious sages throughout the centuries, such as Jesus and Buddha, did not have to insult people or shout at them to get their points across. All of these people can only be called impolite if we define that word as telling the truth to those who don't want to hear it. But the truth can be told with dignity, compassion, and manners.

In everyday life, we all sometimes must do things that seem rude. We may have to sever relations with a romantic partner, fire an unsatisfactory employee, or confront someone who's harming someone else. But all of these can be done with respect for the other person's point of view; any action can be done rudely or kindly, and there's no reason not to choose kindness. Although the person we confront will be hurt or angry, those feelings are tempered, in the long run, by the memory of how the unpleasant event was handled.

In the final analysis, being as polite as possible is the key guideline. It's impossible to avoid ever raising one's voice or upsetting someone; sometimes truths must be told, even when it hurts. But anything that must be done can be done with kindness. Doing so can only make a bad situation better for everyone concerned and add a tiny bit to the harmony of our world.

### Model Sentences of Essay # 25

1. Good manners have virtually disappeared from our self-centered world.

2. People butt into line at the supermarket, guests on

political news shows shout at each other, fist fights break out in the Korean National Assembly.

3. Actually, though, it is better to be as polite as possible in all circumstances, even when that is not the same as never offending anyone.

4. The twentieth century's greatest moral leaders, the people who truly improved the world, conducted themselves with great dignity and politeness.

5. Mahatma Gandhi, Nelson Mandela, and Martin Luther King, Jr. achieved great things by loving their enemies while calmly and politely demonstrating against moral failures.

6. The great religious sages throughout the centuries, such as Jesus and Buddha, did not have to insult people or shout at them to get their points across.

7. In everyday life, we all sometimes must do things that seem rude. We may have to sever relations with a romantic partner, fire an unsatisfactory employee, or confront someone who's harming someone else.

> 26. Does ethical behavior impede the pursuit of success?

"Nice guys finish last," the American baseball manager Leo Durocher famously said, articulating the common belief that it takes unethical behavior—lying, bending the rules, cheating—to win. Although he was talking about a baseball pennant race, people in many walks of life have subscribed to, and secretly followed, his prescription for winning. In the end, though, what *is* success? Becoming rich and famous may or may not require dishonest behavior, but a moral code is not a hindrance to true success, it's an absolute necessity.

First we should examine whether unethical conduct leads to success. For everyone who has achieved their goals through trickery, another has done so by maintaining his moral code. Being honest and reliable leads to trust from others, and a good reputation is a powerful tool to what the world calls "success."

While it's true that many devious people have risen to the heights of society, often they come crashing to the ground. For example, the most famous American baseball players of their era, Mark McGwire, Barry Bonds, and Roger

Clemens, have been revealed as steroid users and liars. They have their millions of dollars, but have lost the respect (and sometimes adulation) of a world of baseball fans. Ken Lay of Enron Corporation died waiting to be imprisoned; Bernie Madoff, who stole hundreds of billions of dollars of his clients' money, will spend the rest of his life in jail. Was it worth it?

What is success, anyway? That, as Hamlet said, is the question. Is it being famous, or rich, or powerful? Those things certainly seem like success to many people. Although people say that money can't buy happiness, it can certainly rent it. It would be more fun to spend the weekend lying on the beach in Hawaii or skiing in the French Alps than trudging from home to work and back again in midwinter. But true success is not about money, or fame, or even happiness. Success is being able to sleep at night and look yourself in the eye in your mirror every morning. It's knowing that you have helped others, that the world is a tiny bit better because you're in it.

Every major religion in the world shares the same message: we are on earth to help each other. Money is nice, but plays a limited factor in bringing about true happiness. Fame is fine, but it fades. Power means always looking over your shoulder to see who wants to take it away. You are not a success unless you have the respect of those around you and, more importantly, of yourself. Success is a clear conscience, a peaceful mind, and someone to love. True success is impossible without morality.

Model Sentences of Essay # 26

1. "Nice guys finish last," the American baseball manager Leo Durocher famously said, articulating the common belief that it takes unethical behavior—lying, bending the rules, cheating—to win.

2. Although he was talking about a baseball pennant race, people in many walks of life have subscribed to, and secretly followed, his prescription for winning.

3. Becoming rich and famous may or may not require dishonest behavior, but a moral code is not a hindrance to true success, it's an absolute necessity.

4. Being honest and reliable leads to trust from others, and a good reputation is a powerful tool to what the world calls "success."

5. For example, the most famous American baseball players of their era, Mark McGwire, Barry Bonds, and Roger Clemens, have been revealed as steroid users and liars.

6. Although people say that money can't buy happiness, it can certainly rent it.

7. It would be more fun to spend the weekend lying on the beach in Hawaii or skiing in the French Alps than trudging from home to work and back again in midwinter.

8. Money is nice, but plays a limited factor in bringing about true happiness.

9. You are not a success unless you have the respect of those around you and, more importantly, of yourself.

10. Success is being able to sleep at night and look yourself in the eye in your mirror every morning.

> 27. What is more reflective of personal character: actions or words?

Do actions or words reveal a person's true attitudes? I'd say it depends. First, everyone perceives the same person differently. Second, people's attitude changes overtime. Even though there can be a consistent pattern in one's behavior, it is extremely difficult to predict it accurately because everyone thinks and acts differently. Eastern and western philosophies discuss similar topics in their texts, as well as contemporary psychologists in the 20th and 21st century.

Many philosophers and scientists have said that one's perspective plays an important role in an observation. For example, Buddha once said, "Those whose mind is rich always finds others rich." Here, he meant that one's view can be skewed depending on the person's state of mind. Hundreds of years later in Europe, David Hume said, "Humans can only perceive what they can pick up from their senses." Such Hume's philosophy can be well explained by our modern day medical science. According to Ramachandran, a contemporary neurologist, human brains contain mirror neurons which help people understand and learn from others through imitation. In other words, if people can relate a behavior that they see to their past experience, they can judge and understand others better. However, if they can't, they might not readily accept or comprehend the person's behavior. Since everyone perceives others' behaviors differently (or see things from their own perspectives), one's true intentions can be read differently.

Secondly, most humans thoughts change naturally according to time and location. This means people's thoughts and emotions may change from time to time, even if they are read correctly. For example, a French philosopher, Jean Paul Sartre's philosophy evolved as he aged. As a young writer, he believed human behavior could be read quite accurately as they think and behave in a pattern. However, by the time he died, he said, "We can only perceive a fragment of what one thinks." An ancient Chinese philosopher, Lao Tsu used to describe a human mind as "the myriad creatures," and I think he explained this complexity very well.

A human mind is just as complicated as our neural structures of the brain. Millions of neurons are inter-connected and they function instantaneously. If one can catch that and distinguish it as "one thought," only then, can he argue that a man's intention or behavior can be read fairly accurately.

## Model Sentences of Essay # 27

1. Even though there can be a consistent pattern in one's behavior, it is extremely difficult to predict it accurately because everyone thinks and acts differently.

2. According to Ramachandran, a contemporary neurologist, human brains contain mirror neurons that help people understand and learn from others through imitation.

3. Since everyone perceives others' behaviors differently (or from their own perspectives), one's true intentions can be read differently.

4. As a young writer, he believed human behavior could be read quite accurately as they think and behave in a pattern.

5. An ancient Chinese philosopher, Lao Tsu used to describe a human mind as "the myriad creatures," and I think he explained this complexity very well.

6. A human mind is just as complicated as our neural structures of the brain.

7. Millions of neurons are inter-connected and they function instantaneously.

> 28. Are lives improved when changes are made?

Our lives get faster and faster, at a faster and faster rate. My father could remember when cars were so rare that if one drove through his village, everyone would run outside to see it. Nobody he knew had a telephone. Now we can travel by train at a speed of one kilometer every twelve seconds and I can talk to my friend 15,000 kilometers away in real time, complete with color video. The communicators in the Star Trek television show a generation ago which were only dreamed of by science fiction writers are now taken for granted, set 400 years in the future, were basically cell phones. Yet, as Mahatma Gandhi said, "There is more to life than increasing its speed." In our rush to modernize, we may have lost as much as we have gained.

Most of our inventions have made our lives easier and faster. Music on vinyl records gave way to cassettes, then to CDs, then to MP3s, calculations with pencil and paper to $200 book-sized, four function calculators to $5 credit-card thin graphing calculators. Generally speaking, our lives are better now in the sense of what we can do and how quickly and easily we can do it. It's good to be able to see an important event live from the other side of the world or he at up our lunches in two minutes. Compared to our parents and grandparents, we have very easy lives indeed.

On the other hand, while the World Wide Web builds bridges to people around the world, technology can build walls between us and our friends an family. For example, I coached cross-country (running) for eight years in the United States. We would rent a van and I would drive seven or eight of my runners to meet in other cities. For the first few years, the trip made the team feel like a family; we exchanged stories, jokes, and thoughts throughout the drive. Suddenly, though, around 2001 or so, all of the runners had MP3 players and handheld video games, and disappeared into themselves five minutes after we left school. In a van full of teenagers, I felt as if I was alone.

The song *Both Sides Now* says, "Something's lost and something's gained in living every day." The natural question in this case is "What have we lost?" We've lost the togetherness of unhurried dinners with our families, the excitement of getting a real letter in the mail, the experience of sitting outside in the evenings watching the kids play baseball. They're all inside, in their separate houses, playing video games. Is what we have gained greater than what we have lost? Maybe.

Model Sentences of Essay # 28

1. Now we can travel by train at a speed of one kilometer every twelve seconds and I can talk to my friend 15,000 kilometers away in real time, complete with color video.

2. Music on vinyl records gave way to cassettes, then to CDs, then to MP3s, calculations with pencil and paper to $200 book-sized, four function calculators to $5 credit-card thin graphing calculators.

3. For the first few years, the trip made the team feel like a family; we exchanged stories, jokes, and thoughts throughout the drive.

4. On the other hand, while the World Wide Web builds bridges to people around the world, technology can build walls between us and our friends and family.

5. Suddenly, though, around 2001 or so, all of the runners had MP3 players and handheld video games, and disappeared into themselves five minutes after we left school.

6. We've lost the togetherness of unhurried dinners with our families, the excitement of getting a real letter in the mail, the experience of sitting outside in the evenings watching the kids play baseball.

7. For the first few years, the trip made the team feel like a family; we exchanged stories, jokes, and thoughts throughout the drive.

> 29. What important qualities are shared by famous or successful people?

Abraham Lincoln and Charles Darwin each did something that perhaps no other person could have done. Lincoln, through his political ability and force of will, kept the United States a unified country and ended 250 years of slavery in America. Darwin went on a five-year voyage and worked for over 20 years to formulate his theory of evolution, which overturned pre-nineteenth century superstition. What Lincoln and Darwin had in common was keen intelligence and fierce will.

Lincoln was a little-known backwoods politician when he ran for president, and then, seemingly, was unexpectedly elected president. His ambition and political skill helped vault him over many more famous candidates. Once he was president, he was resolute in not allowing the Southern states leave the Union. He did not allow the Northern states to stop fighting. It was only his determination that saved the country; perhaps no one else could have done it. He used his intelligence to see the war to its conclusion, speaking eloquently of the cause and, when the time was right, freeing the slaves. Extraordinary times demand extraordinar y men. Lincoln came from the frontier at the exact moment his nation needed him.

Darwin's voyage on *HMS Beagle* took him from England to South America, Africa, and Australia. During those five years, he collected fossils and studied living birds, turtles, and other animals. Drawing especially from his observations in the Galapagos Islands off South America, he began to formulate his theory of evolution. His will led him to devote nearly thirty years of his life to the voyage and to formulating his ideas, and to dare to publish a theory that overturned thousands of years of spiritual belief and outraged religious people worldwide. His intelligence led him to see connections where no one before him had. Darwin is the most important figure in changing our world view from superstition to science.

Both men, Abraham Lincoln and Charles Darwin, shared the quality of having a strong sense of tenacity and bravery. With Darwin, it was his courage to challenge the hitherto established doctrine of creationism. Abraham Lincoln, similarly, had the courage to finally put to question the issue of slavery and solve it once and for all.

## Model Sentences of Essay # 29

1. Lincoln, through his political ability and force of will, kept the United States a unified country and ended 250 years of slavery in America.

2. Darwin went on a five-year voyage and worked for over 20 years to formulate his theory of evolution, which overturned pre-nineteenth century superstition.

3. Lincoln was a little-known backwoods politician when he ran for president, and then, seemingly, was unexpectedly elected president.

4. He used his intelligence to see the war to its conclusion, speaking eloquently of the cause and, when the time was right, freeing the slaves.

5. Drawing especially from his observations in the Galapagos Islands off South America, he began to formulate his theory of evolution.

6. His will led him to devote nearly thirty years of his life to the voyage and to formulating his ideas, and to dare to publish a theory that overturned thousands of years of spiritual belief and outraged religious people worldwide

7. With Darwin, it was his courage to challenge the hitherto established doctrine of creationism.

## 30. What plays a larger role for achieving success: effort or good fortune?

Effort and luck are intertwined in life. They are linked together like a DNA string; effort and luck determine a person's future. Indeed, success in life is earned and a matter of luck.

Obviously, success is an amalgamation of factors. People are more likely to achieve and be successful if they work hard and set goals. The foundation of education is constructed of discipline, diligence and a look toward the future and success. Still, education and all that it entails is not a guaranteed recipe for success. Dedication, personal character and effort may not be enough.

The problem involves the luck of the draw. Life to a great extent is like a poker game and success may depend on the cards dealt to you. Let's look at an example, albeit an extreme one. Clearly, if a child is born in the poorest regions of Africa, or any other third-world country, he will not likely have the same opportunities as young people do in Western nations. In fact, instead of encountering opportunities, people in such forlorn countries often are confronted with misery and devastation. Success, along with education, may be just a concept or dream to them. To state that such people can succeed simply based on the ability to work hard and earn their way is preposterous. On the other hand, to emphasize that luck simply causes the success of a person is just as wrongheaded and perhaps insulting. "I'd never yell 'Good luck!' at anybody," said Holden Caulfield, the protagonist in J.D. Salinger's *The Catcher in the Rye*. "It sounds terrible, when you think about it."

Still another example of luck's power relates to being born into royalty. Does anyone really think that the obvious success of Prince William is much more than luck? From conception, luck has accompanied the presumptive future king of England. Yes, he has studied hard and gone to the best schools. And, his strength of character may well contribute to being an accomplished king one day. But, his success is interwoven with luck.

Having said that, hard work and all those other traits founded in education can lead to success. Again, those qualities are not a guarantee of achievement. However, people who strive and earn their way can be ready for the possibility of success, when it comes through opportunities. Seneca, a Roman philosopher, said in the mid-1st Century AD, "Luck is what happens when preparation meets opportunity."

So, what does it take to be prepared for opportunity? No matter where they are born or live, people must learn and embrace knowledge, whether through formal education or personal experience. People must strive and earn their way in life. Then they will be ready to take advantage of luck, which, perhaps, could come in ordinary forms such as business, professional or educational opportunities. Many successful people will tell you that their achievements in life were due at least in part to luck. They were in the right place at the right time.

Therefore, success in life is earned and a matter of luck. Thomas Jefferson, the third U.S. president, addressed the issue. He said, "I'm a great believer in luck, and I find the harder I work, the more I have of it."

## Model Sentences of Essay # 32

1. They are linked together like a DNA string; effort and luck determine a person's future.

2. Obviously, success is an amalgamation of factors.

3. The foundation of education is constructed of discipline, diligence and a look toward the future and success.

4. Life to a great extent is like a poker game and success may depend on the cards dealt to you.

5. Clearly, if a child is born in the poorest regions of Africa, or any other third-world country, he will not likely have the same opportunities as young people do in Western nations.

6. In fact, instead of encountering opportunities, people in such forlorn countries often are confronted with misery and devastation.

7. On the other hand, to emphasize that luck simply causes the success of a person is just as wrongheaded and perhaps insulting.

8. From conception, luck has accompanied the presumptive future king of England.

9. Then they will be ready to take advantage of luck, which, perhaps, could come in ordinary forms such as business, professional or educational opportunities.

> 31. Do television images of immoral behavior and violence make society immoral and dangerous?

Our lives are saturated with media: television, movies, music, and above all the Internet. Our lives are full of vicious and immoral behavior as well, if not in quantity, then in type; we are seeing new and different types of harmful activities. These facts are not coincidental. There is no doubt that the media contribute to a degradation of morality.

For example, there is a notorious news story in central Florida regarding the murder of a homeless person. The unfortunate homeless person, Mike Roberts, was in his 40s when he was brutally attacked. Having emotional problems, he ended up homeless, relocating to the woods in the Daytona Beach suburb of Holly Hill. In May, 2005, a group of teenagers beat him to death "for fun" and "for something to do."

One of the boys came back repeatedly over several hours to beat the semiconscious man, eventually crushing his skull with a concrete block. At the trial, it came out that several of the boys were avid consumers of videos of homeless people being beaten, and they played the "Grand Theft Auto" video game series, which glorifies casual violence. In the case of the homeless person, the teenagers are a reflection of how television images of immoral behavior and violence make society more dangerous.

In another realm, recent news articles have publicized the trend in Western countries for young people to "hook up", that is, to engage in casual sexual encounters with multiple partners, with no commitment or emotional attachment. Various societies have placed varying degrees of importance on marriage as a prerequisite for sexual behavior, but even contemporary, permissive Western societies have maintained the norm that emotional intimacy should precede physical intimacy. The 'hookup" is a rejection of moral behavior, and is promoted by the modern media, from mainstream movies to the pornography that is readily available on the Internet.

In conclusion, can it be proven that the media contribute to violence and promiscuity? It cannot, if we use the criminal-trial standard of "guilt beyond a reasonable doubt." However, by the standard of common sense, the causality is clear: as young people are exposed to more and more violent, dangerous, and immoral behavior in the media, they are desensitized. What was once taboo is now seen as common, and society's standards are degraded. The media must share the blame.

Model Sentences of Essay # 31

1. Our lives are full of vicious and immoral behavior as well, if not in quantity, then in type; we are seeing new and different types of harmful activities.

2. The unfortunate homeless person, Mike Roberts, was in his 40s when he was brutally attacked. Having emotional problems, he ended up homeless, relocating to the woods in the Daytona Beach suburb of Holly Hill.

3. In May, 2005, a group of teenagers beat him to death "for fun" and "for something to do." One of the boys came back repeatedly over several hours to beat the semiconscious man, eventually crushing his skull with a concrete block.

4. At the trial, it came out that several of the boys were avid consumers of videos of homeless people being beaten, and they played the "Grand Theft Auto" video game series, which glorifies casual violence.]

5. In the case of the homeless person, the teenagers are a reflection of how television images of immoral behavior and violence make society more dangerous.

6. In another realm, recent news articles have publicized the trend in Western countries for young people to "hook up", that is, to engage in casual sexual encounters with

multiple partners, with no commitment or emotional attachment.

7. Various societies have placed varying degrees of importance on marriage as a prerequisite for sexual behavior, but even contemporary, permissive Western societies have maintained the norm that emotional intimacy should precede physical intimacy.

8. The "hookup" is a rejection of moral behavior, and is promoted by the modern media, from mainstream movies to the pornography that is readily available on the Internet.

9. However, by the standard of common sense, the causality is clear: as young people are exposed to more and more violent, dangerous, and immoral behavior in the media, they are desensitized.

10. What was once taboo is now seen as common, and society's standards are degraded.

## 32. Is war sometimes necessary?

The history of humanity is the history of war. There was war in Mesopotamia 5,000 years ago; there is war in Mesopotamia today. The American incursion in Iraq has been fought in the footsteps of the conquerors of Samaria. Must there be war? For humankind, no; we must learn to stop war or, with our modern weapons, we will eventually wipe ourselves out. For individual nations, under special circumstances, the answer is yes and that war is sometimes necessary.

Even the most pacifistic person, if he has any sense, must see that there are times when a country must go to war. In the late 1930s, the Western democracies tried to placate Adolf Hitler's Germany. They ceded country after country to the Nazis, vainly hoping to achieve what British Prime Minister Neville Chamberlain called "peace in our time." The result was, of course, the near-destruction of Europe and the death of twelve million people in the holocaust. The cost, if the democratic world had not eventually confronted Hitler, would have been far higher: the subjugation or death of many more millions of Africans, Asians, and people of any other group that didn't fit Hitler's idea of the

Master Race.

However, the occasions when war is unavoidable are far rarer than many politicians believe. The United States, for example, has fought dozens of wars and isolated campaigns. All too often, these wars have been grounded in greed or racism. The Philippines, Puerto Rico, and large swathes of what is now the American Southwest were seized by the United States in unnecessary wars against "lesser" peoples. Five hundred Native American nations were subjugated and nearly destroyed in decades of genocidal war.

However, many nations are guilty of grabbing all the riches and territory they could by sheer force of arms: from the Roman Empire to the British Empire, from Imperial Japan to the Soviet Union, many countries have used war and the threat of war to enrich themselves, at the cost of millions of lives.

Eventually, though, we must come to the larger questions. Is war necessary to the human race? Is it inevitable? As the novelist Herman Wouk wrote, "We must end war, or it will end us." We simply cannot survive indefinitely as a species that preys upon itself; our military development is millennia ahead of our moral development.

In the end, that is the heart of our dilemma: can we le

arn to live in peace before it is truly, finally too late? The answer is no, not unless we can learn at long last to be at peace in our own hearts. War is caused by the struggle within us, and between us. Abraham Lincoln said, "We are not enemies, but friends. We must not be enemies." We must somehow, as Lincoln said, be touched "by the better angels of our nature." We must not be enemies.

## Model Sentences of Essay # 32

1. The American incursion in Iraq has been fought in the footsteps of the conquerors of Samaria.

2. Even the most pacifistic person, if he has any sense, must see that there are times when a country must go to war.

3. In the late 1930s, the Western democracies tried to placate Adolf Hitler's Germany.

4. The cost, if the democratic world had not eventually confronted Hitler, would have been far higher: the subjugation or death of many more millions of Africans, Asians, and people of any other group that didn't fit Hitler's idea of the Master Race.

5. The Philippines, Puerto Rico, and large swathes of what is now the American Southwest were seized by the United States in unnecessary wars against "lesser" peoples.

6. However, many nations are guilty of grabbing all the riches and territory they could by sheer force of arms: from the Roman Empire to the British Empire, from

Imperial Japan to the Soviet Union, many countries have used war and the threat of war to enrich themselves, at the cost of millions of lives.

7. In the end, that is the heart of our dilemma: can we learn to live in peace before it is truly, finally too late?

> 33. Has today's abundance of information only made it more difficult for us to understand the world around us?

The proliferation of the Internet has made information more abundant and widespread, helping us better understand the world. Before the advent of the Internet, and television, the radio, and newspaper, the rate at which new information spread through society was slow. Before such innovations in media, brilliant ideas were confined to a few circles, requiring interested students to become transient scholars and travel to universities and libraries. If the abundance of information showed educated thinkers the immensity of the world around them, then, it is correct to say today's abundance of information has made it more confusing for people to understand the world around them.

In many branches of philosophy, people who are content with a limited or false perspective of the universe suffer from an illusion. Therefore, today's abundance of information should not be deemed as an information phenomenon with only negative consequences. Many people are able to sift through and tell the difference between junk information and useful information. It is important to have faith in individuals and their ability to digest a diverse set of information and then make a rational conclusion.

Before the growth of media, especially before the Enlightenment period in Europe, gross superstition and ignorance was common. A society lacking a network of information, such as magazines, newspapers, radio, and the Internet, is not equipped with the proper mechanisms to transmit innovative ideas to interested parties and individuals.

Without the proper channels, otherwise intelligent and thoughtful individuals are isolated from one another, reflecting a society with no ability to make significant headway on solving their most pressing social problems.

In conclusion, today's abundance of information has promoted tolerance in people who may have otherwise been more closed minded and discriminatory. Highly educated societies are more tolerant of people from a different race, country, culture, sexual orientation, and religion. The reason for their tolerance is due to their exposure to uncommon (to their social norms) forms of behavior, and this exposure is a form of education. The Internet provides access to a multitude of perspectives. A society without a strong network of information such as television, the radio, and especially the Internet, is limited in their exposure of foreign influences.

## Model Sentences of Essay # 33

1. The proliferation of the Internet has made information more abundant and widespread, helping us better understand the world.

2. Before the advent of the Internet, and television, the radio, and newspaper, the rate at which new information spread through society was slow.

3. If the abundance of information showed educated thinkers the immensity of the world around them, then, it is correct to say today's abundance of information has made it more confusing for people to understand the world around them.

4. In many branches of philosophy, people who are content with a limited or false perspective of the universe suffer from an illusion.

5. Many people are able to sift through and tell the difference between junk information and useful information.

6. Before the growth of media, especially before the Enlightenment period in Europe, gross superstition and ignorance was common.

7. A society lacking a network of information, such as magazines, newspapers, radio, and the Internet, is not equipped with the proper mechanisms to transmit innovative ideas to interested parties and individuals.

8. Without the proper channels, otherwise intelligent and thoughtful individuals are isolated from one another, reflecting a society with no ability to make significant headway on solving their most pressing social problems.

9. In conclusion, today's abundance of information has promoted tolerance in people who may have otherwise been more closed minded and discriminatory.

10. The reason for their tolerance is due to their exposure to uncommon (to their social norms) forms of behavior, and this exposure is a form of education.

### 34. Is courage a human trait that is dormant with little opportunity to be used or demonstrated?

If we define "courage" as the ability to stand against great physical danger, very few of us ever have the chance, or the need, to find out whether we have it. However, there is another kind of courage, the will to persevere and to overcome whatever life throws at us, to do what must be done no matter the cost. We are all called upon to manifest this courage many times throughout our lives.

The stereotypical idea of courage is for someone to risk his life to save others. The Biblical book of John tells us, "Greater love hath no man than this, that a man lay down his life for his friends." Courage, in all its manifestations, is a form of great love, of sacrificing oneself for the welfare of others. Think of the hundreds of members of the *New York Police Department* and the *Fire Department of New York* who went running into the burning World Trade Center buildings and *up* the stairs as everyone else was running down and out—or leaping hundreds of feet to their deaths. There is no greater courage, no greater love, than their actions.

Of course, few of us are lifesavers or war heroes. But the quieter kind of courage, the kind that makes us face wh at we think we can't face for the benefit of someone we love or for a just cause, is something that we can show many times in our lives. The woman with ovarian cancer who goes to work every day, not telling her kids of her condition; the man who works minimum-wage jobs from 8 a.m. to midnight so that his children have decent meals; the citizen who stands up and tells the world hard to voice honesty and withstands the abuse she gets for it—these people show true courage as well. Sudden death is not the only demon that needs courage to face down. Even the timid little boy who presents his first elementary-school book report is courageous. Most people undergo blips of courage in their lifespan.

How would any one of us act if asked to risk his life to save others? Fortunately, most of us will never find out. Courage, of course, is not the lack of fear, but the will to act despite our fear. That is something we must do many times in our lives. Courage is indeed a common human trait; if you know where to look, you can see it manifested every day.

## Model Sentences of Essay # 34

1. If we define "courage" as the ability to stand against great physical danger, very few of us ever have the chance,

or the need, to find out whether we have it.

2. We are all called upon to manifest this courage many times throughout our lives.

3. Courage, in all its manifestations, is a form of great love, of sacrificing oneself for the welfare of others.

4. But the quieter kind of courage, the kind that makes us face what we think we can't face for the benefit of someone we love or for a just cause, is something that we can show many times in our lives.

5. Sudden death is not the only demon that needs courage to face down.

6. Most people undergo blips of courage in their lifespan.

7. Courage, of course, is not the lack of fear, but the will to act despite our fear.

> 35. Should people plan for good things to happen to them, or should they depend on the idea of destiny to bring good fortune?

Sometimes the time is ripe for a person to achieve greatness. Senator Barack Obama, given his Muslim father, his inexperience, and his skin color, could never have been elected president at any other time in American history. Disgust with the Bush administration and a ravenous desire for change opened the door of the White House to the most unlikely winner ever. But Obama did not wait until conditions were ideal; he moved forward, and then the wheels of fate aligned in his favor. If he had waited until the time was right, he would not have had time to mount an effective campaign.

The first problem with waiting for opportunity is that it might never come. If someone expects the door to achievement to swing open one day, he may discover too late that the door is stuck. Rather, great things are achieved when he takes every opportunity he is given. First, Obama won election to the Illinois state senate; then he gained overnight fame when he delivered a stirring keynote address at the 2004 Democratic National Convention. Next he won electio n to the U.S. Senate, from which he staged his amazingly successful presidential campaign. He said yes to every opportunity that came along; he didn't wait for everything to be just right.

Perhaps the secret to success lies not in waiting for destiny, but in seeing it around every corner, behind every door. This may, in fact, be the same thing as simply making our own breaks. The founders of Internet sites such as Google, Twitter, and Facebook did not wait; they saw a chance, took it, and are all now multimillionaires. The world didn't know it needed a massive online auction site, but the founder of eBay did. He did not wait for a door to swing open; he blasted his way through a wall.

When Disraeli wrote, "Everything comes if a man will only wait," he was mistaken. The only thing that is sure to come if a man only waits is death. Anything good in life must be pursued, not waited for.

## Model Sentences of Essay # 35

1. Disgust with the Bush administration and a ravenous desire for change opened the door of the White House to the most unlikely winner ever.

2. If someone expects the door to achievement to swing open one day, he may discover too late that the door is stuck.

3. He gained overnight fame when he delivered a stirring keynote address at the 2004 Democratic National Convention.

4. Perhaps the secret to success lies not in waiting for destiny, but in seeing it around every corner, behind every door.

5. The founders of Internet sites such as Google, Twitter, and Facebook did not wait; they saw a chance, took it, and are all now multimillionaires.

6. The world didn't know it needed a massive online auction site, but the founder of eBay did.

7. He did not wait for a door to swing open; he blasted his way through a wall.

> 36. Do you believe the love of money is the root of all evil?

The seventeenth-century King James Bible translation tells us that the love of money is the root of all evil. All we have to do to disprove this is to point out some evils that were not caused by avarice; we can look at Adolf Hitler, Kim Il-Sung, and Charles Manson. However, more accurate, twentieth-century translations of the Bible read "…the love of money is the root of all *kinds of* evil", and that unquestionably is true.

For example, Bernard Madoff turned a $5000 investment into a multi-billion dollar Wall Street financial firm. His desire for money drove him to develop a Ponzi scheme, that is, a plan to make investors believe that they were receiving returns for their money. In reality, the money was not actually being invested; Madoff was pocketing it. In December 2008, the Federal Bureau of Investigation arrested him, acting on a tip from his two sons. His senseless desire for more, and still more, money assured that he will spend his old age in jail. What was the point? Can one live any better with 27 billion dollars than with one billion?

Actually, studies show that, once basic survival needs are met, someone's financial worth has very little effect on his happiness. We carry our outlook on life with us, and the subjective experience of earning $300 a week and wanting to make $400 is much the same as that of making $30,000 a week and wanting to bring home $40,000. When greed takes hold, however much we have is never enough. In some people, the insane desire for more money leads to lying, embezzlement, betrayal, sometimes even murder.

The Biblical aphorism is often misquoted as "money is the root of all evil." That is far from the truth; money is a good thing. It represents what we contribute to the world and it allows us to feed, clothe, and house ourselves and our families, and to buy things that bring us pleasure. There is no shame in money, or in wanting it. But the love of money—that is, putting it before everything else—is the root of all kinds of evil indeed.

Model Sentences of Essay 36

1. His desire for money drove him to develop a Ponzi scheme, that is, a plan to make investors believe that they were receiving returns for their money.

2. For example, Bernard Madoff turned a $5000 investment into a multi-billion dollar Wall Street financial firm.

3. His desire for money drove him to develop a Ponzi scheme, that is, a plan to make investors believe that they were receiving returns for their money.

4. His senseless desire for more, and still more, money assured that he would spend his old age in jail.

5. Actually, studies show that, once basic survival needs are met, someone's financial worth has very little effect on happiness.

6. In some people, the insane desire for more money leads to lying, embezzlement, betrayal, sometimes even murder.

But the love of money—that is, putting it before everything else—is the root of all kinds of evil indeed

> 37. Are memories of past events central to understanding ourselves?

Memory, Luis Bunuel writes, "…is our coherence, our reason, our feeling… without it, we are nothing." Memory indeed helps make us who we are. But slavish devotion may hinder progress. Memory is the background of the self-portrait we paint every day, but what matters is the figure in the foreground: who we are now. We must never be so absorbed in the background that we forget to focus on today.

For example, I have always defined myself in a certain way: intelligent and funny, but often cripplingly shy, both of strangers and of new situations. I have many years of memories of not going to parties, not jumping off the high diving board, not speaking up in a crowd. I piled up decades of memories of saying no to anything new and challenging. The self-definition, the behavior, and the accumulated memories all fed on each other in a seemingly endless loop. Memory reinforced my self-portrait.

Then, last year, I came to a crossroads in my life, an unexpected nothing-to-lose moment that made me consider doing something that even six months before would have shocked me. I began applying for teaching jobs in Korea. I had never thought of committing myself to a culture so foreign to my own, with what is for Americans a very difficult language, among people I knew so little about. It took a tremendous leap of faith—even getting to Korea required setting aside my memories of being afraid to fly.

Thus far, my stay in Korea has been a very positive one, largely because now I act the way I want to be, not the way I always have. We cannot just turn off our memories, but sometimes we need to set them aside, to keep them from defining who we are.

The point is that memories define us to ourselves, both in good and bad ways, and sometimes that can be terribly limiting. What matters is the present; the past is gone, and memory can be both a blessing and a curse. It isn't within our power to forget what's happened, but we must be able, when it helps us to do so, to put the past where it belongs: in the past.

Model Sentences of Essay # 37

1. Slavish devotion may hinder progress.

2. Memory is the background of the self-portrait we paint every day, but what matters is the figure in the foreground:

who we are now.

3. I have many years of memories of not going to parties, not jumping off the high diving board, not speaking up in a crowd.

4. The self-definition, the behavior, and the accumulated memories all fed on each other in a seemingly endless loop.

5. I came to a crossroads in my life, an unexpected nothing-to-lose moment that made me consider doing something that even six months before would have shocked me.

6. It took a tremendous leap of faith—even getting to Korea required setting aside my memories of being afraid to fly.


7. We cannot just turn off our memories, but sometimes we need to set them aside, to keep them from defining who we are.

> 38. Does the road to success or to failure involve pleasing people?

There is no aspect of a human being that is more valuable than his individuality. Trying to please everyone is a sure route to conformity and mediocrity. People who have made their mark in the world—more importantly, people who live happy lives—are people who are not afraid to be themselves. As the American singer Rick Nelson sang, "You can't please everyone, so you got to please yourself."

The first objection to the idea of pleasing everyone is that it is utterly impossible. No matter what you do, there will be people who disapprove of your actions. For example, in the month after the attacks on the World Trade Center and the Pentagon, President George W. Bush's approval rating in the United States was an astonishing 86 percent; now, ten days before he leaves office, it rests at 25 percent.

A lot of water has gone under the bridge (and over New Orleans) since 2001, and events have naturally undermined his popularity. The point, though, is that even during the flag-waving frenzy after 9/11, one in seven Americans didn't like him, and even now, with America at its lowest ebb since the 1930s, one in four does.

Even trying to please the vast majority of people does not work. An author, film maker, or musician may try to tailor her work to popular taste, and may in fact reach limited success; the line from Spice Girls to Wonder Girls is a short one. But nobody reaches artistic greatness or long-lasting success without originality. Moreover, in compromising one's own vision for the sake of popularity, the individual loses a bit of what makes him who he is: a unique individual, never seen before and never to be seen again.

Finally, the question comes down to whether we want to be second-rate imitations of what others want (or rather, what we *think* others want) or first-rate versions of ourselves. In the end, each of us has to live with himself, and to like the person he lives with. As St. Paul wrote in the Bible, "What does it profit a man to gain the whole world and lose his soul?" We must not forfeit who we are and what we believe to try to please the mythical "everyone."

## Model Sentences of Essay # 38

1. Trying to please everyone is a sure route to conformity and mediocrity.

2. People who have made their mark in the world—more importantly, people who live happy lives—are people who are not afraid to be themselves.

3. The point, though, is that even during the flag-waving frenzy after 9/11, one in seven Americans didn't like him, and even now, with America at its lowest ebb since the 1930s, one in four does.

4. Moreover, in compromising one's own vision for the sake of popularity, the individual loses a bit of what makes him who he is: a unique individual, never seen before and never to be seen again.

5. An author, film maker, or musician may try to tailor her work to popular taste, and may in fact reach limited success; the line from Spice Girls to Wonder Girls is a short one.

6. Finally, the question comes down to whether we want to be second-rate imitations of what others want (or rather, what we think others want) or first-rate versions of ourselves.

7. We must not forfeit who we are and what we believe to try to please the mythical "everyone."

> 39. Do you believe the criteria for justice is set and molded only by the strong and victorious?

Cynics may agree with Thrasymachus but I do not. While I am certain that there was much truth to his statement in the ancient times he lived in, I feel the human race has advanced morally. Today, many governments are established, at least in part, to protect all of their citizens from the harm that those with more strength, but fewer morals, might inflict. The developed countries have mostly tried to create independent judiciaries to implement an even-handed justice system.

It is true that throughout much of human history the principle of "might makes right" held true. The men of the Roman Empire felt they had the right to conquer as much of the world as they could. So too, did Genghis Khan and many others. In fact, my country, America, was settled by Europeans who felt it was their right to take the land even if it meant killing the native population.

However, we do make progress in morality and ethics much like we do in science and technology. We feel appalled by the actions of our ancestors and predecessors. The world's reaction to the Nazis is telling. The Nuremberg Trial show an interest in protecting the weak from the stronger. We have progressed beyond the point that "Justice is nothing more than the interest of the stronger."

In conclusion, as human history has shown, the strong and victorious parties often do decide the fate of justice. However, as human civilization advance to contemporary notions of justice, a more fair and balance approach to prosecution and justice has supplanted past forms of prosecution.

## Model Sentences of Essay # 39

1. Today, many governments are established, at least in part, to protect all of their citizens from the harm that those with more strength, but fewer morals, might inflict.

2. The developed countries have mostly tried to create independent judiciaries to implement an even-handed justice system.

3. It is true that throughout much of human history the principle of "might makes right" held true.

4. We feel appalled by the actions of our ancestors and predecessors.

5. The Nuremberg Trials show an interest in protecting the weak from the stronger.

6. We have progressed beyond the point that "Justice is nothing more than the interest of the stronger."

7. However, as human civilization advance to contemporary notions of justice, a more fair and balance approach to prosecution and justice has supplanted past forms of prosecution.

> 40. Do we detest the flaws in others that we see in ourselves?

Reserving special scorn for others who demonstrate our own character flaws is the height of hypocrisy. Why should we blame someone for succumbing to the same weaknesses that we ourselves indulge in? However, while we can usually count on what Mark Twain called "the damned human race" to be hypocritical, do we in fact come down harder on someone indulging in our own weaknesses? The fact is that we don't.

For example, consider a particular type of bigotry born of fear. In 1942, President Franklin Roosevelt ordered the internment of all Americans of Japanese ancestry living on the west coast. These people, some of them third- and fourth-generation American citizens, lost everything they owned and spent years imprisoned in old army bases and horse stalls. In the 80s, some called for the internment of people with HIV. After the attacks of September 11, some demanded the internment of Arab-Americans. Are the people who wanted this the same people who decried the racism of six decades ago? They are not. Rather, many are the same people who excused and rationalized the Japanese internm ent. More rational people condemn the prejudice of 1942, of 1982, and of 2001.

What about animal-rights advocates? Are they so adamant about the cruelties visited on defenseless animals—calves raised for slaughter under horrifying conditions, dogs beaten by their owners, laying hens, their beaks and toes chopped off, crowded twenty to a cage—because they themselves are brutal people? The opposite is true; they are dedicated to kindness, almost unanimously opposed to needless violence.

We must insert a word of caution: everyone's heart contains some prejudice, some violence, some of every sin: sloth, lust, greed, and the rest. Perhaps we are, to a degree, put off when we see others indulging themselves in our own worst flaws. This demonstrates our hypocrisy. But often we excuse in others what we excuse in ourselves and resent people who demonstrate the flaws of which we ourselves have only a trace.

## Model Sentences of Essay # 40

1. Reserving special scorn for others who demonstrate our own character flaws is the height of hypocrisy.

2. Why should we blame someone for succumbing to the same weaknesses that we ourselves indulge in?

3. These people, some of them third- and fourth-generation American citizens, lost everything they owned and spent years imprisoned in old army bases and horse stalls.

4. Perhaps we are, to a degree, put off when we see others indulging themselves in our own worst flaws.

5. But often we excuse in others what we excuse in ourselves and resent people who demonstrate the flaws of which we ourselves have only a trace.

6. We must insert a word of caution: everyone's heart contains some prejudice, some violence, some of every sin: sloth, lust, greed, and the rest.

7. Perhaps we are, to a degree, put off when we see others indulging themselves in our own worst flaws.

## 41. Should society censure some kinds of information or forms of expression?

Who decides what other people may see, read, or say? The very concept of censorship is based on the idea that there is an authority wiser than the individual, and that it has the right, even the duty, to keep others from harming themselves with such subversive activities as thought. But who grants it that right? The answer is: nobody. Authority abrogates the right, confidently assuming that it is wiser and more sophisticated than ordinary citizens. The government is neither God nor parent, and often what it prevents people from seeing is material that would challenge its own power.

The greatest societies are those that accord freedom to their people. The United States Constitution's First Amendment is a beautifully concise statement of the duty of a government to allow its people the first human right, the right to think: "Congress shall make no law respecting an establishment of religion, or prohibiting the free exercise thereof; or abridging the freedom of speech, or of the press; or the right of the people peaceably to assemble, and to petition the Government for a redress of grievances." This is th e bedrock of the modern world's first free society.

Censorship is a slippery slope; at the bottom lie Hitler's Germany, Mao's China, and Big Brother's Oceania from *1984*. But government does not need to be fascist to limit its people's freedom, and the authorities (governmental, educational, or religious) are notoriously poor judges of art: among the most often banned and censored works are such masterpieces as Twain's *Huckleberry Finn*, Joyce's *Ulysses*, and Salinger's *Catcher in the Rye*. Another word for censorship is bowdlerization, after the Reverend Thomas Bowdler, who literally took scissors to the sections of Shakespeare that he found offensive.

The story of the human race is of a long slog toward freedom. Censorship is the attempt of the powerful to limit the thought of the powerless. It is arrogant and self-serving. Once again we must ask of the powerful, who gives you that right?

## Model Sentences of Essay # 41

1. The very concept of censorship is based on the idea that there is an authority wiser than the individual, and that it has the right, even the duty, to keep others from harming themselves with such subversive activities as thought.

2. Authority abrogates the right, confidently assuming that it is wiser and more sophisticated than ordinary citizens.

3. The greatest societies are those that accord freedom to their people.

4. But government does not need to be fascist to limit its people's freedom, and the authorities (governmental, educational, or religious) are notoriously poor judges of art: among the most often banned and censored works are such masterpieces as Twain's Huckleberry Finn, Joyce's Ulysses, and Salinger's Catcher in the Rye.

5. Another word for censorship is bowdlerization, after the Reverend Thomas Bowdler, who literally took scissors to the sections of Shakespeare that he found offensive.

6. The story of the human race is of a long slog toward freedom.

7. Censorship is the attempt of the powerful to limit the thought of the powerless.

> 42. Is it always advantageous to pool the efforts and traits of people to reach the most effective solution for any given problem?

Different cultures place varying emphasis on the importance of independence versus interdependence. For example, the American ideal is the lone wolf, the self-sufficient loner who goes his own way and needs no one. On the other hand, the Japanese have a saying, "The tall nail gets hammered down." In other words, anyone who tries to stand alone will learn that he is only one of the crowd. Korean culture teaches the primacy of family, the duty of interdependence within a small, specific group. In reality, though, interdependence is a necessity for any advances in a culture.

In the United States, the concept of independence is so crucial to the country's identity that the word appears in its founding document. Even the Declaration of Independence, however, concludes with the phrase "… we mutually pledge to each other our Lives, our Fortunes and our sacred Honor." The most famous emblem of the rebellion against Britain was a flag showing a snake divided into thirteen segments, each labeled with the name of a colony, and the imperative "Join or Die." Benjamin Franklin famously said

, "Gentlemen, we must hang together or most assuredly we shall hang separately." Even the world's most notoriously individualistic country would not exist if it had not followed Franklin's declaration of interdependence.

But what about innovators, scientists, and explorers? The people who have made our lives what they are today are equally dependent on each other. Isaac Newton famously said, "If I have seen further it is only by standing on the shoulders of Giants." All advancements are made through collaboration, whether with present partners or past pioneers. Without Galileo, there would have been no Newton; without Newton, no Einstein or Hawking. Barack Obama would not have been elected as the United States' most unlikely President without the contributions of millions of people.

Even great artists rely on others; it is often forgotten that Shakespeare was a friend of Ben Jonson and Christopher Marlowe, and took most of his plots from other playwrights and historians. J.R.R. Tolkien was a reader of C.S. Lewis' *Chronicles of Narnia* and Lewis of Tolkien's *Lord of the Rings*. The Beatles would have been nothing without the artistic contributions of Buddy Holly and American blues artists or the behind-the-scenes efforts of manager Brian Epste in and arranger George Martin.

In the final analysis, as the old saying goes, "None of us knows as much as all of us." To put it another way, whether it is an artistic or scientific collaboration, a family, a team, or a nation, the whole is always greater than the sum of the parts. We need each other.

## Model Sentences of Essay # 42

1. Different cultures place varying emphasis on the importance of independence versus interdependence.

2. For example, the American ideal is the lone wolf, the self-sufficient loner who goes his own way and needs no one.

3. Even the world's most notoriously individualistic country would not exist if it had not followed Franklin's declaration of interdependence.

4. All advancements are made through collaboration, whether with present partners or past pioneers.

5. Barack Obama would not have been elected as the United States' most unlikely president without the contributions of millions of people.

6. The Beatles would have been nothing without the artistic contributions of Buddy Holly and American blues artists or the behind-the-scenes efforts of manager Brian Epstein and arranger George Martin.

7. The most famous emblem of the rebellion against Britain was a flag showing a snake divided into thirteen segments, each labeled with the name of a colony, and the imperative "Join or Die."


8. To put it another way, whether it is an artistic or scientific collaboration, a family, a team, or a nation, the whole is always greater than the sum of the parts. We need each other.

### 43. Does comparison with others allow people to appreciate what they have as individuals?

People are always comparing their possessions with others. At age four, a child will be delighted with a box of 32 crayons… until the kid next door has 64; at forty-four, a man may think that a Toyota Camry looks pretty sharp in his driveway… until his neighbor pulls up in a new Lexus. It's a natural human tendency to want more than the next guy. But it does not have to be that way. My little iPod Shuffle is still great, even if my friend has an iPhone.

First, we don't need much to appreciate what we do have. "The best things in life are free," the old song says, and it's true. Love, sunlight, humor: the best things don't depend on our having money. Harvard professor Tal Ben-Shahar, in his bestselling book *Happier*, quotes studies that show that, once basic survival needs are met, those of modest means are as happy as the rich. Sheryl Crow sings, "It's not having what you want, it's wanting what you've got." The purpose of having a mansion or a yacht is not to have the physical object, but to be happy. Maybe we don't need the material goods; what if we just learned to be happy?

Going back a bit further than Sheryl Crow, the Tenth Commandment states "Thou shalt not covet thy neighbor's house, thou shalt not covet thy neighbor's wife, nor his manservant, nor his maidservant, nor his ox, nor his ass, nor any thing that is thy neighbor's." Clearly, wanting what the next guy has is nothing new. But because an impulse is natural, is it inevitable? In another religious tradition, the Buddha taught that Nirvana comes in letting go of all desire. In material terms, the less we have, the less concerned we are with what our neighbor has, the freer we are. Not having means not worrying about keeping; not wanting means not wanting more.

Finally, we need to recognize that many human impulses, such as greed, anger, lust, and envy, can have disastrous consequences. It should mean nothing to us that we see someone with a newer car or a thicker wallet. If it does in fact bother us, the fault lies not in our belongings, but in ourselves. Shouldn't all of us need to make a sound choice at some point, like Erich Fromm says in his book, "To have or to be."

## Model Sentences of Essay # 43

1. It is a natural human tendency to want more than the next guy.

2. Harvard professor Tal Ben-Shahar, in his bestselling book Happier, quotes studies that show that, once basic survival needs are met, those of modest means are as happy as the rich.

3. Going back a bit further than Sheryl Crow, the Tenth Commandment states "Thou shalt not covet thy neighbor's house.

4. But because an impulse is natural, is it inevitable?

5. In material terms, the less we have, the less concerned we are with what our neighbor has, the freer we are.

6. We need to recognize that many human impulses, such as greed, anger, lust, and envy, can have disastrous consequences.

7. Shouldn't all of us need to make a sound choice at some point, like Erich Fromm says in his book, "To have or to be."

> 44. Should long-standing systems of behavior deserve to remain in existence because they are established traditions?

A woman sits in a church pew in Baltimore, silently mouthing "The peace of the Lord be with you" along with the priest, unable to fulfill the destiny she was born for, to express her faith by being a priest herself. Another woman, in Kabul, is unable to leave the house unless she is accompanied by a male relative and every inch of her body but her eyes is covered. A third, in Kashmir, is murdered by her husband's relatives because her father did not pay a sufficient dowry. Not all traditions deserve to survive; the survival of some traditions means the death of human freedom.

The idea that all traditions should continue indefinitely is ludicrous. All traditions were born, whether from science or superstition, faith or fear, to serve some purpose of a society. Most, but not all, traditions made sense at some point in the past. But conditions change, thought evolve, and society grows. What seemed sensible in 1776 or 1865 may not appear so reasonable in 2008, and we cannot be shackled by what someone thought centuries, or even decades, ago.

This is not to say that traditions should be tossed aside lightly; many of them have served us well. Some, such as the Golden Rule, are the basis for our laws and reflect the human dignity we claim to accord all people. Chuseok in Korea and Thanksgiving in the United States bring families together for fellowship and food. Every nation has its patriotic holidays, when love of country unites all citizens. For the most part, traditions are good and necessary things.

But to disprove the concept that "all established holidays deserve to remain in existence", one need only name one that doesn't deserve to live on. Here are five: slavery, apartheid, suttee (ritual, voluntary burning to death of Hindu widows), human sacrifice, and (on a less lethal scale) blue laws making it illegal for stores to be open on Sunday. Any tradition, whether familial, religious, or national, may have originated due to good or bad motives; for the most part, the ones that have survived have proven to be positive. But there are far too many exceptions to the rule, and each tradition should be evaluated by succeeding generations to see if it still makes sense. To do less is to be prisoners of the past.

## Model Sentences of Essay # 44

1. Another woman, in Kabul, is unable to leave the house unless a male relative accompanies her and every inch of her body but her eyes are covered.

2. A third, in Kashmir, is murdered by her husband's relatives because her father did not pay a sufficient dowry.

3. All traditions were born, whether from science or superstition, faith or fear, to serve some purpose of a society.

4. What seemed sensible in 1776 or 1865 may not appear so reasonable in 2008, and we cannot be shackled by what someone thought centuries, or even decades, ago.

5. Some, such as the Golden Rule, are the basis for our laws and reflect the human dignity we claim to accord all people.

6. But to disprove the concept that "all established holidays deserve to remain in existence", one need only name one that doesn't deserve to live on.

7. Any tradition, whether familial, religious, or national, may have originated due to good or bad motives; for the most part, the ones that have survived have proven to be positive.

8. But there are far too many exceptions to the rule, and each tradition should be evaluated by succeeding generations to see if it still makes sense.

---

45. Have modern advancements improved the quality of people's lives?

Modern advancements have improved the quality of people's lives significantly. In contemporary times, underdeveloped regions in the world suffer from low life expectancy rates, high infant mortality rates, and high death rates due to preventable diseases. Moreover the United Nations consistently ranks developed nations as being much happier than underdeveloped nations.

Contemporary nations with extreme poverty mirror the past economic conditions of industrialized nations. For example, medieval Europe exhibits the economic and health standards of many contemporary poor nations. The life expectancy of Europeans in the medieval era was roughly at 30 years of age. This is a similar range for contemporary sub-Saharan Africans who do not presently benefit from modern advancements in medicine that had helped raise the life expectancy of the developed world.

Advancements in medicine have markedly improved the lives of people living in developed nations. The infant mortality rate (number of deaths per 1,000 births) in the OECD is less than 5 deaths. In underdeveloped nations, the rate increases to 80 deaths and, in extremely underdeveloped regions in Sub-Sahara Africa, the infant mortal rate is well over 110 deaths. High infant mortality rates reflect, in part, the general happiness of the population, with better prospects for births being a boon to human populations as they naturally hinge their happiness to strong and big family.

There may be sufficient arguments discounting the effectiveness of comparing developed and underdeveloped nations, but the United Nations has developed a comprehensive strategy for measuring the happiness of nations. Called the World Happiness Report, the United Nations measures the happiness of nations according to a diverse set of indicators. The report does not measure countries by only their GDP per capita, but also based on their level of good governance, income disparity, poverty, income gap and so forth. Field agents are sent to every country where which details surveys are conducted. The result of the United Nations findings are telling: People in developed nations are consistently happier than people in underdeveloped nations. It appears that, according to the quality expertise from the folks at the United Nations, certain modern advancements in medicine and economy improves the quality of people's lives significantly.

In conclusion, modern advancements have improved the quality of lives in the fields of social equality, medicine, and governance. Not only are health statistics in favor of modern advancements, but also the idea is supported by worldwide acclaimed surveys such as the one conducted by the United Nations.

Model Sentences of Essay # 45

1. In contemporary times, underdeveloped regions in the world suffer from low life expectancy rates, high infant mortality rates, and high death rates due to preventable diseases.

2. Contemporary nations with extreme poverty mirror the past economic conditions of industrialized nations.

3. For example, medieval Europe exhibits the economic and health standards of many contemporary poor nations.

4. This is a similar range for contemporary sub-Saharan Africans who do not presently benefit from modern advancements in medicine that had helped raise the life expectancy of the developed world.

5. In underdeveloped nations, the rate increases to 80 deaths and, in extremely underdeveloped regions in Sub-Sahara Africa, the infant mortal rate is well over 110 deaths.

6. There may be sufficient arguments discounting the effectiveness of comparing developed and underdeveloped nations, but the United Nations has developed a comprehensive strategy for measuring the happiness of nations.

7. The report does not measure countries by only their GDP per capita, but also based on their level of good governance, income disparity, poverty, income gap and so forth.

8. Field agents are sent to every country where which details surveys are conducted.

9. It appears that, according to the quality expertise from the folks at the United Nations, certain modern advancements in medicine and economy improves the quality of people's lives significantly.

10. Not only are health statistics in favor of modern advancements, but also the idea is supported by worldwide acclaimed surveys such as the one conducted by the United Nations.

46. Are politicians, by virtue of being public figures, under pressure to succeed?

As prime minister of England during World War II, Winston Churchill provided bold leadership and rousing inspirational speeches to lead his people through a terrible chapter in history. He said later, "The price of greatness is responsibility," as an attempt to explain the pressure great leaders and public figures are burdened by. In this essay I will examine the expectations of a population, and whether or not we expect too much from our public figures. For this case, I will define greatness as the actions of a single individual who has achieved something significant for the benefit of the larger population. As well, responsibility is the pressure inherent to the position of representing the needs and opinions of the population. Today, people expect too much from leaders because we are led to believe that these people are capable of touching our lives beyond the realities of their public office.

First, the realistic expectations of a leader are very simple and greatness is attainable for those who fulfill their duty. We should expect that a person seeking public office is doing so in order to accurately and fairly represent the nee ds and opinions of the people he is responsible for, and not following a more personal agenda. In this way, one can expect that a leader guides the state in the direction of the majority opinion, and does not sway from the general moral principles of the society. Obviously, the leader cannot make decisions that all people agree with, but must be trusted not to make a decision that may put citizens in danger or risk the overall security or economic stability of the nation. These expectations of our public figures are realistic, but today the ideal of greatness is undergoing a metamorphosis.

Today, to be chosen for high public office requires an incredible amount of money and media exposure, and it is in this process where we are losing the simplicity of Churchill's statement. While campaigning for office, candidates inevitably characterize themselves as tremendously powerful and ready to do whatever it takes to improve the lives of each citizen. Clearly this is impossible and untrue, yet as this web of perfection is spun through advertisements, interviews, speeches, and debates, we begin to raise our own expectations to this ludicrous plateau established by politicians. Citizens begin talking about candidates as if we know them personally, and we become interested in their personal lives. However, once the voting process is over, we find that within months the reality sets in that there will actually be very little change at all in our daily lives, regardless of who won the election. In this way, our expectations are built up to impossible heights and then quietly dissolved as we invariably see our leaders making decisions that we disagree with. Eventually, our expectations drop to match the reality of the public offices, and we finally admit that what we have is just another distanced leader. It is this process of courting voters which leads us to be inherently let down by our public figures.

A current example of this media-blurred political phenomenon is the on-going presidential race in the United States. Mass communication via internet and television has afforded voters with a round the clock update of events involving the candidates, as well as the details of each wavering opinion poll and the endless reaction of people in the media. This process is so long and arduous that every possible angle of each candidate is held up to the light and examined. As this process deepens, we begin to detach from reasonable expectation of what our potential leader will do, and we fill it in with trivial likes or dislikes about the individual's personality. The problem increases as the candidates begin addressing issues such as the economy, while giving the i mpression that our lives could be improved quickly and simply, all by voting for them. These are the kind of impossible promises of greatness that later fall flat and leave people feeling a bit duped by the intensity and passion of media attention. When the flurry subsides, we will likely have become even more embittered by the democratic process and not knowing what we should expect from our leaders at all.

Finally, we see that the matter of our expectations for greatness is a delicate balance between the representatives and those being represented. Indeed, in a world where exacting information has become so readily available, the notion of personal privacy for those in the public spotlight. People seem to be limitless in our capacity for entertainment and information, and the business of politics has become just one more form of social enticement. It seems that today the most important issues have more to do with wearing the right tie at a speech or the perfect "framing" of a new candidate's family. However, despite this muddying of the idea of "responsibility," there are still great things being accomplished by great men and women in many nations. Perhaps the new measure of greatness is to take on first the responsibility of media, and then once established, continue o n to do great things for the people.

Model Sentences of Essay # 46

1. As prime minister of England during World War II, Winston Churchill provided bold leadership and rousing inspirational speeches to lead his people through a terrible chapter in history.

2. In this way, one can expect that a leader guides the state in the direction of the majority opinion, and does not sway from the general moral principles of the society.

3. Today, to be chosen for high public office requires an incredible amount of money and media exposure, and it is in this process where we are losing the simplicity of Churchill's statement.

4. Clearly this is impossible and untrue, yet as this web of perfection is spun through advertisements, interviews, speeches, and debates, we begin to raise our own expectations to this ludicrous plateau established by politicians.

5. Mass communication via internet and television has afforded voters with a round the clock update of events involving the candidates, as well as the details of each wavering opinion poll and the endless reaction of people in the media.

6. As this process deepens, we begin to detach from reasonable expectation of what our potential leader will do, and we fill it in with trivial likes or dislikes about the individual's personality.

7. These are the kind of impossible promises of greatness that later fall flat and leave people feeling a bit duped by the intensity and passion of media attention.

8. When the flurry subsides, we will likely have become even more embittered by the democratic process and not knowing what we should expect from our leaders at all.

9. Finally, we see that the matter of our expectations for greatness is a delicate balance between the representatives and those being represented.

10. Perhaps the new measure of greatness is to take on first the responsibility of media, and then once established, continue on to do great things for the people.

47. Can fame be the bearer of happiness, or are people who are not famous more likely to be

In every society there are individuals who have climbed into the lime-light for a number of different reasons. Some famous people are artists and entertainers, while some are known as great athletes or business moguls. We are naturally intrigued by the lives of celebrities, and it is easy to assume that they are eternally happy with their fame. However, we often see famous people who are unhappy. In this essay, I will compare the lives of the famous and non-famous in order to determine a difference in happiness. For this purpose, happiness is defined as a consistent positive feeling of satisfaction and fulfillment due to the accomplishment of a goal or goals. Although celebrities and normal people lead different lifestyles, there is no difference between their potential for happiness. I will explain this concept in the following pages.

First, the idea or position of happiness can be very simple, yet many people struggle in search of it every day. If we look at happiness as something anyone can attain, then whether someone is famous or not makes no difference. However, as a society we tend to heavily associate happiness with wealth, public successes, and stability. For this reason, those most famous for these qualities become the ideal of happiness in our minds. The rich and famous people we see in the media fascinate our imaginations and lead us to envy their elevated position. But are they really happier than ourselves? Using the definition of happiness outlined above, we see that this notion of inherent "celebrity happiness" is a fallacy of our glittering popular culture.

Most people who become famous work very hard to do so, but are not necessarily happier than other people. Following the drive to become famous is a difficult path, and it requires a certain amount of luck, as well as talent and determination. When a person achieves fame, it does not guarantee happiness because fame alone is not sustainable. As a hardworking individual reaches the point of name recognition and broad public interest in society, this is a success. However, once at this point, they must continue living each day and setting new goals in order to be happy with their lives.

There are several examples of celebrities who have been unable to sustain their sanity and stability after reaching a social position of intense public exposure. An interesting case is the crumbling of Britney Spears' fame in recent year

s. As the world watched, she fell from being one of the most popular and successful performers in history to a collapsed persona experiencing the breakup of her marriage and family and her simultaneous mental breakdown. For years her image was that of the ideal, "All-American Girl Next Door," but we see now that she was in fact tormented by the same self-doubt and dissatisfaction in life that we all can face each day. She said once, "On stage I'm the happiest person in the world. Off stage I'm just like everybody else." As her appeal began to dwindle, we can see why the cracks appeared as they did. Because her happiness was based on the success of her career, it is no wonder she fell apart when her career cooled off.

In conclusion, happiness is a point which anyone can reach, whether they are famous or not. To assume fame inherently rewards one with long term happiness is false, because we often see those in the spotlight who have lost all happiness. It is truer to say that any person is capable of finding and maintaining their own level of satisfaction, regardless of social position and public exposure. The real secret to being happy is to simply understand what one wants and needs, and to work each day towards those rewards. However, though this may be the logical key to unlocking sati sfaction in our common lives, we will no doubt continue to be dazzled by the beautiful and successful people who color our popular culture.

Model Sentences of Essay # 47

1. Some famous people are artists and entertainers, while some are known as great athletes or business moguls.

2. For this purpose, happiness is defined as a consistent positive feeling of satisfaction and fulfillment due to the accomplishment of a goal or goals.

3. Using the definition of happiness outlined above, we see that this notion of inherent "celebrity happiness" is a fallacy of our glittering popular culture.

4. There are several examples of celebrities who have been unable to sustain their sanity and stability after reaching a social position of intense public exposure.

5. As the world watched, she fell from being one of the most popular and successful performers in history to a collapsed persona experiencing the breakup of her marriage and family and her simultaneous mental breakdown.

6. For years her image was that of the ideal, "All-American Girl Next Door," but we see now that she was in fact tormented by the same self-doubt and dissatisfaction in life that we all can face each day.

7. However, though this may be the logical key to unlocking satisfaction in our common lives, we will no

doubt continue to be dazzled by the beautiful and successful people who color our popular culture.

## 48. Is the world changing for the better?

While the world is far from realizing its utopian dreams, I do believe that the world is changing for the better, ever so slowly, based on few significant strides made.

Firstly, our current society recognizes a larger scope of basic human rights than we have done so in the past. It was not of such a distant past that we justified slavery as a morally acceptable means of operation. While the historical immediacy of slavery still haunts us as it did Roland Barthes when he gazed into a black and white photograph of a once enslaved man, we also celebrate the social movements that protested against the act of owning another man. Even the greatest achievements of ancient civilizations, when studied with the acknowledgment of enslaved labor, do not seem so splendid and aggrandizing. After 300 years of horrific infliction, America finally made progress noteworthy enough in illustrating its original founding concepts as laid down in the Declaration of Independence.

Moreover, while the sad affair of Earth's natural environment illustrates too well our short-sighted fixations on *the profitable*, ecological awareness has been gaining more attention. Much efforts on "green" innovations have been m ade in the last five years, and the ever increasing number of hybrid automobile manufacturers illustrates this perfectly. Although bad conventions of industrialization cannot be remedied overnight, the recognition of the need for change marks a significant step toward a more sustainable living.

Finally, in order to implement and improve upon these slow-moving reformations, we must approach the future with an optimistic outlook and generate enough energy to support the efforts made in the right direction.

Therefore, based on the actual progress made toward creating a better world in addition to the positive changes yet to come, we must believe that the world is indeed changing for the better, not in order to stagnate in the backwater of complacency, but rather to practice the true meaning of "looking towards the future."

### Model Sentences of Essay # 48

1. It was not of such a distant past that we justified slavery as a morally acceptable means of operation.

2. While the historical immediacy of slavery still haunts us as it did Roland Barthes when he gazed into a black and white photograph of a once enslaved man, we also celebrate the social movements that protested against the act of owning another man.

3. After 300 years of horrific infliction, America finally

made progress noteworthy enough in illustrating its original founding concepts as laid down in the Declaration of Independence.

4. Much effort on "green" innovations has been made in the last five years, and the ever increasing number of hybrid automobile manufacturers illustrates this perfectly.

5. Although bad conventions of industrialization cannot be remedied overnight, the recognition of the need for change marks a significant step toward a more sustainable living.

6. Finally, in order to implement and improve upon these slow-moving reformations, we must approach the future with an optimistic outlook and generate enough energy to support the efforts made in the right direction.

7. In order to cease from stagnating in the backwater of complacency, we should practice the true meaning of "looking towards the future."

> 49. A conscience is a powerful motivator, but is it more influential than money, fame, or power?

I, like most people, do not deny my desire for money, fame and power, but I also firmly believe that it is not necessary to forgo of one's own conscience in order to acquire the riches.

While we have numerous examples of political and religious martyrs sacrificing their own welfare for a cause or a principle they deem more important than their own lives, I do not feel it is necessary, or beneficial even, to set up a binary position, putting conscience and personal interest on opposing ends. On the contrary, one should be encouraged to affirmatively consider and acknowledge conscience as a key factor in obtaining one's desired treasures.

Hastily dismissing greed as an evil trait would only instigate a guilty conscience, which in most cases leads either to moral escapism or self-denial convincing us to initially repress our needs and desires only to later hide our shameful acts of self-interest. On the other hand, blindly accepting avarice as an innate human characteristic also proves problematic, because it will give rise to a society of utter chaos and the actualization of a 'dog-eat-dog' world.

Inspired to decipher a personal position on this misinterpreted Darwinism, I conducted a sociological experiment while attending graduate school. I attempted to reach a state of "deficit" by randomly approaching people on streets with an offer to exchange their quarter (25¢) for my dollar ($1). If succeeded, I would experience a loss of 75¢, while the participant would gain 75¢ from the interaction. I carried out this experiment on 15 subjects at different settings and times, as well as with various attires to manipulate the impressions I would have on the participants.

Although I do have to admit to the initial bias, or faith, in human generosity, I was happily astonished when all who were approached gladly gave up their quarter instead of accepting my dollar in exchange. Every person politely refused my insistence on taking the dollar for the generosity. While this humble experiment did not turn the world upside down or discredit all notions of cynicism, it marked a tiny feat of faith in human kindness for me.

Thus, I fervently believe in a synergistic approach to education where encouragement, rather than punishment, is utilized to deepen our morals and ethics so that the guiding voice of conscience may help us envision a society of humans 'more human than human' beyond the clutch of the pleasure principle.

<u>Model Sentences of Essay # 49</u>

1. We have numerous examples of political and religious martyrs sacrificing their own welfare for a cause or a principle they deem more important than their own lives.

2. I do not feel it is necessary, or beneficial even, to set up a binary position, putting conscience and personal interest on opposing ends.

3. Hastily dismissing greed as an evil trait would only instigate a guilty conscience, which in most cases leads either to moral escapism or self-denial convincing us to initially repress our needs and desires only to later hide our shameful acts of self-interest.

4. On the other hand, blindly accepting avarice as an innate human characteristic also proves problematic, because it will give rise to a society of utter chaos and the actualization of a 'dog-eat-dog' world.

5. Inspired to decipher a personal position on this misinterpreted Darwinism, I conducted a sociological experiment while attending graduate school.

6. Although I do have to admit to the initial bias, or faith, in human generosity, I was happily astonished when all who were approached gladly gave up their quarter instead of accepting my dollar in exchange.

7. While this humble experiment did not turn the world upside down or discredit all notions of cynicism, it marked a tiny feat of faith in human kindness for me.

> 50. Are the greatest griefs in life those that we cause ourselves?

The quote by Sophocles, one of the greatest Greek tragedians, refers to an opinion that griefs, which we cause ourselves, are brought about by our own choices, and therefore, are more difficult to endure. I agree with this statement because it teaches us the importance of facing up to the consequences for the acts we commit, and thus, assists in establishing free will as an utmost human condition. It touches upon the seemingly contradictory relationship between free will and fatalistic determinism, and is perfectly illustrated through the tragedy of Oedipus Rex, one of the three Theban plays, written by none other than Sophocles himself.

Oedipus, the main protagonist of the play, achieves wealth and power until suddenly falling to destitution as a consequence for the series of acts that he commits. He is born into the world with an oracle of Apollo at Delphi prophesizing his fate to someday kill his father and marry his mother. Upon obtaining this knowledge, the King of Thebes, Oedipus' father, pierces his infant son's feet and orders him to be killed. However, the baby is found and rescued by a shepherd, who names him Oedipus, or "swollen-feet" an d not having the means to raise the child himself, gives the baby to the childless King and Queen of Corinth, who raise him as their own.

Oedipus as a young man also learns of the Delphic Oracle and firmly believing himself to be the true son of the Corinthian King and Queen, decides to escape the disastrous fate by leaving Corinth. On the road to Thebes, however, Oedipus encounters his true father. Unconscious of each other's identities, they fall into an argument which leads to Oedipus murdering the King of Thebes, and thus, fulfilling the first part of the prophesy. Soon after, he solves the riddle of the Sphinx and as a reward, is offered the kingdom of Thebes as well as the hand of the Theban queen, his biological mother. With this, the oracle is inescapably fulfilled.

Further, as a consequence of the murder of the former Theban King, the city falls into a plague and Oedipus, the present King, curses the murderer and vows to avenge the death at all cost without realizing himself to be the cause. Ignoring numerous warnings from those around, Oedipus' pride and unyielding desire to uncover the truth about the former King's murder and the mystery surrounding his own birth, lead him to the tragic realization of his horrific deeds. Upon the final discovery, he blinds himself as punishm ent for his inability to see the truth. While his fate had been determined by the Oracle upon his birth, his own actions are what ultimately lead to his tragic downfall. And the knowledge that the feeling of free-agency and pride are what had led to his actions haunts and torments Oedipus more than of being a helpless puppet to the god's prophesy.

Tragedies and thus, sorrows visit our lives, sometimes even too frequently. However, what Sophocles' quote reminds us is not that we must face and endure these griefs, but that we must choose carefully for we will ultimately pay the price for the choices made. Through the demise of our tragic hero, Oedipus, Sophocles shows us so poignantly that the sorrows we bring ourselves are beyond doubt the most heartfelt, because then, we have no one else to blame but ourselves.

## Model Sentences of Essay # 50

1. The greatest griefs are those we cause ourselves.

2. It touches upon the seemingly contradictory relationship between freewill and fatalistic determinism.

3. The baby is found and rescued by a shepherd, who names him Oedipus, or 'swollen-feet.'

4. On the road to Thebes, Oedipus encounters his true father.

5. He solves the riddle of the Sphinx and, as a reward, is offered the kingdom of Thebes.

6. With this, the oracle's prophesy is inescapably fulfilled.

7. His own actions are what ultimately led to his tragic downfall.

8. Tragedies and sorrows visit our lives, sometimes too frequently.

9. In life, we must choose carefully for we will pay for the choices we make.

10. Oedipus, Sophocles shows us so poignantly that the sorrows we bring ourselves are beyond doubt the most heartfelt, because then, we have no one else to blame but ourselves.

## 51. Does effort lead to success more than luck?

A successful life may certainly be attributed to luck, granted one condition; that is, the acknowledgement of the fact that there is no such thing as *mere* chance. While there is much to be said about the boons of being at the "right place at the right time," upon close observation of such a situation, one will often find that the circumstances in a person's life were probably already foretelling some big break or approaching change. Individuals tend to consistently elicit certain behaviors from others, derive benefit or harm from various situations, and generally appreciate or deride their lot in life based on their dispositions; in doing so, they make their own luck.

This is a philosophical idea that has been given much consideration in many traditions around the world. The Buddhists give this concept the name Karma. Karma is often used, mistakenly, as a synonym for the word "luck." The true meaning however, goes much deeper. The idea of Karma is that, essentially, whatever decisions a person makes come back around. So it follows that if you are an exceptionally lucky person, it is not a matter of coincidence; somehow, you have earned your place in the world.

In scrutinizing my own life, which I believe has had many lucky turns, I realize that every moment that appeared to be a lucky surprise was actually just the next logical step, though one that I did not have the foresight to anticipate. For example, for almost a year, I had a job working at a clothing store. At first I really enjoyed it because the company was very hip and the job was easy and fun, but after a while, the glamour faded, and my grievances at the lack of intellectual stimulus and proper compensation prompted me to consider looking for different work.

One day I was visiting galleries in the art district, just spending a quiet day off without bothering about my current problems. I stopped by a gallery where the owner happened to be a former employer of mine, just to see what he was up to, and to see the current exhibition. As it turned out, he was looking for a manager for his gallery and had not gotten around yet to advertising the position. I walked out of there with a new job and in awe of my good luck.

Yes, I was in the right place at the right time, no question. In retrospect however, it becomes clear that this was not just dumb luck. First of all, the person who hired me had worked with me before. He knew that I was intelligent, hard-working, and knowledgeable in the field. Second, altho ugh I was not planning on soliciting a job, looking back, I am sure that I was subconsciously motivated to stop by this particular gallery, out of the hundreds of others because I was beginning to think about what possible connections I had, and who could help me find a better job. Why else would I show up there at that particular point in time, after a five year hiatus? It was not a particularly enticing exhibition, that's for sure.

In conclusion, success is something you must make for yourself. It is primarily a result of merit, effort, and a good attitude. I believe in the value of having luck on your side, just as long as you understand that you make your own luck.

Model Sentences of Essay # 51

1. While there is much to be said about the boons of being at the "right place at the right time," upon close observation of such a situation, one will often find that the circumstances in a person's life were probably already foretelling some big break or approaching change.

2. Individuals tend to consistently elicit certain behaviors from others, derive benefit or harm from various situations, and generally appreciate or deride their lot in life based on their dispositions; in doing so, they make their own luck.

3. In scrutinizing my own life, which I believe has had

many lucky turns, I realize that every moment that appeared to be a lucky surprise was actually just the next logical step, though one that I did not have the foresight to anticipate.

4. At first I really enjoyed it because the company was very hip and the job was easy and fun, but after a while, the glamour faded, and my grievances at the lack of intellectual stimulus and proper compensation prompted me to consider looking for different work.

5. Second, although I was not planning on soliciting a job, looking back, I am sure that I was subconsciously motivated to stop by this particular gallery, out of the hundreds of others because I was beginning to think about what possible connections I had, and who could help me find a better job.

6. In conclusion, success is something you must make for yourself. It is primarily a result of merit, effort, and a good attitude.

7. I believe in the value of having luck on your side, just as long as you understand that you make your own luck.

## 52. What qualities define heroism and courage?

"I disapprove if what you say, but I would defend to the death your right to say it," the French philosopher Voltaire said. That is a noble sentiment, but not one that many people actually follow. People who stand up and tell what they see as the truth, despite all pressure to stay silent, are often heroes of the highest kind.

Power, in particular, is intolerant of opposition. Fifteenth-century English martyrs were burned at the stake for translating the Bible from Latin into English. Freedom Riders were murdered in Mississippi for daring to say that black Americans should be allowed to vote. An unknown man stood in front of a line of tanks in Tiananmen Square in Beijing and has not been heard of since. Many have paid a heavy price for speaking up for their principles. It requires a toughness of mind and a grace of spirit, sometimes even great nobility and courage, to speak your truth when the world tells you that you're wrong, foolish, or even evil.

On a very small scale, I have seen this myself. On March 15, 2003, in St. Augustine, Florida, university students protested against the impending American invasion of Iraq. They were among two or three dozen people carrying American flags, peace symbols, and signs opposing the Bush administration's plans for an unprovoked attack on Iraq. St. Augustine is a very conservative, pro-military town, and during an hour's protest, many people driving by shouted obscenities, made obscene gestures, and shouted that the students were traitors or terrorists. The city police stopped one young man from jumping out of his pickup truck and beating one of the protestors. Four days later, America was at war.

Although the students may not be considered heroes (they were in no real danger), it took certain strength for them to stand there under the barrage of hatred. It's hard to imagine the moral courage required to put one's life or freedom on the line for the truth. Of course, it must be remembered that heroism depends on what the individual is standing up for; racists, warmongers, and maniacs have also stood for their beliefs despite governmental pressure and public opinion. However, those who risk everything for what is right and what is true are heroes in every sense of the word.

## Model Sentences of Essay # 52

1. That is a noble sentiment, but not one that many people actually follow.

2. People who stand up and tell what they see as the truth, despite all pressure to stay silent, are often heroes of the highest kind.

3. Fifteenth-century English martyrs were burned at the stake for translating the Bible from Latin into English.

4. It requires a toughness of mind and a grace of spirit, sometimes even great nobility and courage, to speak your truth when the world tells you that you're wrong, foolish, or even evil.

5. St. Augustine is a very conservative, pro-military town, and during an hour's protest, many people driving by shouted obscenities, made obscene gestures, and shouted that we were traitors or terrorists.

6. However, those who risk everything for what is right and what is true are heroes in every sense of the word.

7. It must be remembered that heroism depends on what the individual is standing up for; racists, warmongers, and maniacs have also stood for their beliefs despite governmental pressure and public opinion.

## 53. Does fame contribute to happiness?

Nowadays being a celebrity is not reserved for just a few successful musicians or actors. Most successful people, including business people, designers, writers, chefs, and so on, must deal with the benefits and detriments of fame. Many people work hard to work their way up to the top, while others, such as Paris Hilton, the Osbourne kids, or Sean Lennon, are just born into already rich and famous families. The success of any endeavors does not solely depend on the originator's status. Certainly being famous is a useful head start, however, although I agree that the endeavors of famous people are more likely to be recognized at first, I don't think this guarantees that they will succeed.

The key to a successful project is a strong plan, a creative approach, and of course, talent. Now, although they might argue the contrary, celebrities are not necessarily talented, or intelligent. Some of them are merely lucky, rich, or just very charismatic and good at social networking. Although these things may have earned them celebrity status, this does not guarantee that whatever sort of products or ideas they try to get out into the world will be paid any attention to by the general public.

Paris Hilton is a perfect example of this type of incidental celebrity. Many people wonder where she came from and why she is so famous. Well, she was born into the Hilton Hotel empire, and being young, quite rich, and not too smart, she went out, drank too much, and ran around NY and LA doing stupid things. This landed her in the media and her debaucherous lifestyle caught the imagination of many tabloid journalists and bored celebrity-watchers around the world. When she tried to take advantage of this attention by doing an MTV reality show with a friend, the show only achieved moderate success and was soon cancelled. Then, she tried to start a career as a pop musician. Needless to say, that attempt was a flop as well. Her sister, on the other hand, who receives much less attention in the media, runs a successful business designing accessories such as handbags.

Another issue regarding the endeavors of famous people is that someone who has already proven themselves in their field is held to higher standards. For example, when I read books by new writers, I don't have any expectations. I am just as open to being impressed as I am to being disappointed, so I am more willing to be flexible and perhaps mo re lenient in my judgment. When I read a book by a writer that I am already familiar with, however, I am fully expecting it to live up to my preconceived notions. In other words, if I love this person's previous work, and think that the writing is brilliant, I would expect no less from the newer work, and would therefore be a much harsher judge of it.

Fame obviously helps people to get their work noticed, but it's not enough for an endeavor to be lasting or successful. For that, the endeavor must be supported by business sense, creativity, and talent. Sometimes fame can even be harmful, because people have certain expectations from famous people. Many celebrities were originally unknowns like everyone else. They became famous because of their endeavors, and not the other way around. And finally, it has been proven time and again that famous but untalented people's endeavors are likely to fail.

## Model Sentences of Essay # 53

1. Most successful people, including business people, designers, writers, chefs, and so on, must deal with the benefits and detriments of fame.

2. The success of any endeavor does not solely depend on the originator's status.

3. Paris Hilton is a perfect example of this type of

incidental celebrity.

4. This landed her in the media and her debaucherous lifestyle caught the imagination of many tabloid journalists and bored celebrity-watchers around the world.

5. I am just as open to being impressed as I am to being disappointed, so I am more willing to be flexible and perhaps more lenient in my judgment.

6. Fame obviously helps people to get their work noticed, but it's not enough for an endeavor to be lasting or successful.

7. For that, business sense, creativity, and talent must support the endeavor.

> 54. Does the public expect too much from public figures?

In the 1990s, the national spotlight was concentrated on Bill Clinton and allegations of extramarital affairs. At the time, it appeared the public was more concerned with the personal life of the president than his actual policies. The same phenomenon could be said about Barack Obama and questions over his religious faith. Other public figures, notably Jimmy Carter, faced public scrutiny over matters that were completely unavoidable. These historical examples indicate that the public does indeed expect too much from public figures.

Positive economic figures and a landslide victory in his re-election were not enough to prevent Bill Clinton's personal life from entering the spotlight. Major news networks such as CNN and Fox News devoted large segments of their programming to report on Bill Clinton's adulterous behavior. Such national media attention was not spawn solely by journalists and corporate media heads. They responded to public demand and, in this instance regarding Bill Clinton and his personal life, the public essentially mandated further broadcasting and attention. The media frenzy surround ing the controversy is an example of how the public expects too much from public figures, requiring them to be perfect both at work and home.

Similar to Bill Clinton, Barack Obama faced and continues to face unnecessary media attention over his faith. Although repeatedly admitting his Christian faith, there are many in the American public who discount his confession as political maneuvering. Indeed many in the public believe the president is a closeted Muslim by virtue of his father being a foreign born Kenyan. Despite the first amendment, in which the "Separation of Church and State is inviolable", and despite that faith and religion are personal matters, there are large swathes of the American public who continue to point the spotlight on Obama's personal life, damaging his reputation among sympathetic crowds.

The public in the 1970s also indulged in petty politics by putting too much emphasis on Jimmy Carter's personality and foreign affairs. In the late 1970s, the American economy, as well as the global economy in general, was undergoing high inflation and poor economic growth. This was, in part, due to the Middle Eastern crisis between Israel and the Arab nations, which was a conflict the United States could not enter or interfere. Jimmy Carter had little control o ver oil prices sky-rocketing due to the Organization of Petroleum Exporting Countries (OPEC) and their intention to cripple international support for Israel. National support for Jimmy Carter plummeted when the economy nosedived. Here was an example of how foreign affairs, dynamics outside the control of the executive office, unfairly damaged Jimmy Carter's public image. His smooth speaking, calm personality were viewed as the culprit for the nation's economic ills.

In conclusion, there are many events in history which proves that the public expect too much from public figures. Individuals in office are famous, typically graceful, and with that outer shell, many expect them to be perfect. Perfection in all forms to the extent that, minor personal details of their lives, or unavoidable foreign factors, are enough for the public to scrutinize public officials.

## Model Sentences of Essay # 54

1. Positive economic figures and a landslide victory in his re-election were not enough to prevent Bill Clinton's personal life from entering the spotlight.

2. Major news networks such as CNN and Fox News devoted large segments of their programming to report on Bill Clinton's adulterous behavior.

3. Such national media attention was not spawn solely by journalists and corporate media heads.

4. Although repeatedly admitting his Christian faith, there are many in the American public who discount his confession as political maneuvering.

5. Indeed many in the public believe the president is a closeted Muslim by virtue of his father being a foreign born Kenyan.

6. Despite the first amendment, in which the "Separation of Church and State is inviolable", and despite that faith and religion are personal matters, there are large swathes of the American public who continue to point the spotlight on Obama's personal life, damaging his reputation among sympathetic crowds.

7. The public in the 1970s also indulged in petty politics by putting too much emphasis on Jimmy Carter's personality and foreign affairs.

8. Jimmy Carter had little control over oil prices skyrocketing due to the Organization of Petroleum Exporting Countries (OPEC) and their intention to cripple international support for Israel.

9. National support for Jimmy Carter plummeted when the economy nosedived.

10. His smooth speaking, calm personality were viewed as the culprit for the nation's economic ills.

---

55. Does struggle make us value our success and achievements?

Although people proportion the value of things according to energy released, I do not believe that value as a sentiment arises only if effort is expended. There are many things and ideas that are valuable and yet little effort is required to attain them. However in spirit of the question, there is a noticeable relationship between expended effort and associated value. In basic economic philosophy, the demand and scarcity of an object will equal its relative value.

Value in the economic sense may also be applied to a person exhausting their valuable time and resources to produce a specific good, which is obviously scarce to the person who is expending (relatively scarce) energy in exchange for a final good. Conversely, a free good would not be valued as much as a costly good. Since people do value many things, it is logical to assume objects and ideas that are most valuable are those things that require sacrifice.

Goods that are not scarce will likely have a lower value. Least valuable are free goods, despite whether it is important. Take, for example, oxygen and life. Without oxygen many earth organisms would cease to exist, including human beings. It would, then, strike to reason that human beings would highly value oxygen. But people do not get caugh t in a trance and stare at the ceiling while pontificating the value of oxygen because oxygen is a resource abundant good. On the other hand, people who practice scuba diving as a sport, or astronauts in space, do value oxygen. Before entering the sea, scuba divers must mitigate their losses and take with them into the sea a few items so as not to increase their weight, sacrificing goods and experiences in exchange for oxygen. Abundant oxygen and scarce oxygen is an example of how people will approximate their value for things according to their scarcity and biological needs.

Despite the strong influence of scarcity and associated value, human biological needs will not always take into account the value of scarce goods. In other words, the simplest and cheapest things in life may also be the most important and in demand. Materialist philosophers, especially embryonic communists like Hegel, believed that 19th century European farmers turned industrial worker had forsaken more important aspects of life, which had tended to be simple and easy to attain, for rampant materialism that brought no intrinsic value. Nineteenth century rural croppers migrating to the city did so to earn higher wages, precipitating the hitherto unforeseen breakdown of family and society, as materialists philosophers tend to harp about. The relatively stress free lifestyle of the farmer was, according to anti-industrialist thinkers, a better deal than leading a modern life style and being consumed by materialism.

In conclusion, there is a noticeable relationship between the value of things and effort expended to achieve those things. But effort put forth to produce a good does not always equal a proportionate value. Human biological needs do not demand goods in a linear spectrum, setting the price and value according to a reliable framework. Instead there is a complex negotiation between biological needs, and lifestyle and cultural choices with individual uniqueness vis-a-vis the scarcity of goods.

## Model Sentences of Essay # 55

1. Positive economic figures and a landslide victory in his re-election were not enough to prevent Bill Clinton's personal life from entering the spotlight.

2. Major news networks such as CNN and Fox News devoted large segments of their programming to report on Bill Clinton's adulterous behavior.

3. Such national media attention was not spawn solely by journalists and corporate media heads.

4. Although repeatedly admitting his Christian faith, there are many in the American public who discount his confession as political maneuvering.

5. Indeed many in the public believe the president is a closeted Muslim by virtue of his father being a foreign born Kenyan.

6. Despite the first amendment, in which the "Separation of Church and State is inviolable", and despite that faith and religion are personal matters, there are large swathes of the American public who continue to point the spotlight on Obama's personal life, damaging his reputation among sympathetic crowds.

7. The public in the 1970s also indulged in petty politics by putting too much emphasis on Jimmy Carter's personality and foreign affairs.

8. Jimmy Carter had little control over oil prices sky-rocketing due to the Organization of Petroleum Exporting Countries (OPEC) and their intention to cripple international support for Israel.

9. National support for Jimmy Carter plummeted when the economy nosedived.

10. His smooth speaking, calm personality were viewed as the culprit for the nation's economic ills.

56. Does the current system of education promote the acquisition of knowledge, or does it persuade students to conceal their lack of knowledge?

The present system of education encourages people to conceal their lack of knowledge due to social survivalism and egoism. Although the innate search for learning and the acquisition of truth is strong among the human race, spawning the idealist philosophy behind education as an institution, the unfortunate factor here is that people do value their social position more so than their academic position.

There are many who display a pattern of pedantic behavior in order to win over potential rivals and to forge social alliances. Such behavior is attributed to the relationship of the ego to society. The present system of education is also used as a tool for social and natural survival. As a result of the human social condition, the present system of education puts too much pressure to demonstrate the acquisition of knowledge.

Since truth is vast and so widespread, it is not surprising that humanity is unable to capture all of it, and yet the current education system encourages people to conceal their academic weakness. The pressure to demonstrate the acq uisition of knowledge, for example to cite authors from many generations ago, and at the same time to understand the essence of their complicated philosophy is not expected. Perhaps the situation is due to the inability of college exams to gauge the ignorance of a student. A college exam with multiple choice questions does not typically provide the option "Mark if unknown" because students would rather randomly choose an answer with a 25 percent chance of being correct in order to survive. This is a case where lack of honesty by students who interact with expectations from educators leads to the creation of the current education system. Lack of honesty from students, attempts to survive academically and therefore socially, is one reason why the education system encourages us to demonstrate the acquisition of knowledge.

Adding to the interplay of factors, the education system encourages people to conceal their ignorance because people are constantly protecting their ego. The ego here is not altogether related to social survivalism, and therefore the relationship between the education system and the ego deserves a separate thread for discussion. When a student randomly selects a multiple choice answer in hopes of landing the correct answer, that student also hopes for social valida tion. A teacher formatting the exam knows full well the paradigm of test taking and student ignorance. A teacher understands the vast majority of students are also seeking academic validation not just from participants of the education system like instructors, but also from friends, family, and social rivals, which is not conducive for creating an ideal setting. Not only students but also and especially politicians, attorneys, and even instructors themselves often employ pedantic language with the deliverance of their speech for the sole intent on impressing their audience. Here is an example where people are expected to demonstrate their knowledge and, if necessary, their ignorance and lack of knowledge on any given topic and yet fall short for sake of their ego.

In conclusion, the education system encourages us to demonstrate the acquisition of knowledge because there is no other option when dealing with human beings. Students will always safeguard their social position and their ego before becoming perfect stewards to the education system. The condition of humanity therefore makes it inevitable that the present education system would encourage us to conceal our ignorance.

Model Sentences of Essay # 56

1. Although people proportion the value of things according to energy released, I do not believe that value as a sentiment arises only if effort is expended.

2. But people do not get caught in a trance and stare at the ceiling while pontificating the value of oxygen because oxygen is a resource abundant good.

3. Before entering the sea, scuba divers must mitigate their losses and take with them into the sea a few items so as not to increase their weight, sacrificing goods and experiences in exchange for oxygen.

4. Abundant oxygen and scarce oxygen is an example of how people will approximate their value for things according to their scarcity and biological needs.

5. Materialist philosophers, especially embryonic communists like Hegel, believed that 19th century European farmers turned industrial worker had forsaken more important aspects of life, which had tended to be simple and easy to attain, for rampant materialism that brought no intrinsic value.

6. The relatively stress free lifestyle of the farmer was, according to anti-industrialist thinkers, a better deal than leading a modern life style and being consumed by materialism.

7. Nineteenth century rural croppers migrating to the city did so to earn higher wages, precipitating the hitherto unforeseen breakdown of family and society, as materialists philosophers tend to harp about.

8. Human biological needs do not demand goods in a linear spectrum, setting the price and value according to a reliable framework.

9. Instead there is a complex negotiation between biological needs, and lifestyle and cultural choices with individual uniqueness vis-à-vis the scarcity of goods.

> 57. Should the gas emissions of nation-states be tracked by an international monitoring

Nations should have their gas emissions tracked by an international monitoring organization. Because global warming, if indeed an atmospheric phenomenon, is a worldwide issue, it is important that every nation's footprint is proportionate to their geographical and population size. There are non-industrialized nations that contribute little to nothing in greenhouse gas emissions and yet stand to suffer an equal share from the speculated devastating effects of global warming. Since there are some (industrialized) nations releasing the bulk of greenhouse gas emissions suspected of causing global warming, it is to the interest of every nation, despite their carbon footprint, to erect an international agency assigned to monitor greenhouse pollutants ejected by each country. Global warming skeptics mostly believe the structural reforms necessary to reduce greenhouse gas emissions are not worth the costs, opting instead to continue with the status quo.

If global warming is a real, currently transpiring atmospheric phenomenon, there should be steps taken by the international community to halt the unnatural warming of the earth. Since some nations emit more pollutants than others, it therefore becomes important that each nation hold each other accountable for their contribution to global warming. Burnt coal exhaust fumes pumped into the atmosphere from Germany, Chile, or rapidly industrializing China and India also affects the climates of guiltless non-industrial regions of the world. This is why an international agency tracking the gas emissions of each country should be built.

Opponents erecting an international agency to monitor global warming often claim in their set of arguments that penalizing nations would be too costly to both the developed and underdeveloped world. Cost effectiveness for battling global warming is what caused former United States President George W. Bush to reject the Kyoto Protocol, which is a United Nations protocol set to battle global warming through a series of penalties levied on a perpetrating nation. Skeptics such as President George W. Bush believe that, not only is there little data to support global warming as being an actual phenomenon or man-made, but also the economic repercussions of restructuring an economy to be more green friendly far outweighs the supposed benefits of reform.

In conclusion, I believe there should be an internatio

nal agency designed to track each nation's greenhouse gas emissions. Due to the disproportionate role each nation has on the buildup of carbon dioxide in the earth's atmosphere, there should be an internationally recognized agency tracking every country's contribution to global warming. Opponents believe that, because economic costs accompanying industrial reforms are too high, and because global warming could perhaps be mere speculation and not backed by hard scientific data, the status quo ought to remain. I disagree with global warming opponents because it is best to be safe than sorry, with a losing bet in this case spelling far higher economic and human costs.

## Model Sentences of Essay # 57

1. Because global warming, if indeed an atmospheric phenomenon, is a worldwide issue, it is important that each nation's footprint is proportionate to their geographic and demographic size.

2. There are non-industrialized nations that contribute little to nothing in greenhouse gas emissions and yet stand to suffer an equal share from the speculated devastating effects of global warming.

3. Since there are some (industrialized) nations releasing the bulk of greenhouse gas emissions suspected of causing global warming, it is to the interest of every nation, despite

their carbon footprint, to erect an international agency assigned to monitor greenhouse pollutants ejected by each country.

4. If global warming is a real, currently transpiring atmospheric phenomenon, there should be steps taken by the international community to halt the unnatural warming of the earth.

5. Opponents erecting an international agency to monitor global warming often claim in their set of arguments that penalizing nations would be too costly to both the developed and underdeveloped world.

6. Burnt coal exhaust fumes pumped into the atmosphere from Germany, Chile, or rapidly industrializing China and India also affects the climates of guiltless non-industrial regions of the world.

7. Skeptics such as President George W. Bush believe that, not only is there little data to support global warming as being an actual phenomenon or man-made, but also the economic repercussions of restructuring an economy to be more green friendly far outweighs the supposed benefits of reform.

8. Global warming skeptics mostly believe the structural reforms necessary to reduce greenhouse gas emissions are not worth the costs, opting instead to continue with the status quo.

9. Opponents believe that, because economic costs accompanying industrial reforms are too high, and because global warming could perhaps be mere speculation and not backed by hard scientific data, the status quo ought to remain.

10. Due to the disproportionate role each nation has on the buildup of carbon dioxide in the earth's atmosphere, there should be an internationally recognized agency tracking every country's contribution to global warming.

> 58. Does a strong desire for technological attainment cause a society to neglect other values, such as education and the protection of the environment?

A strong commitment for technological progress in a society tips the scale of social priorities by causing fundamental values such as education and environmentalism to be neglected. Rampant materialism in a society does not appreciate the stimulus to the human soul that which is provided by non-material things. A plastic product does not nourish the belief in sustaining nature, but instead it further destroys the forests, woods, mineral deposits and other environmental sources that help produce these technological products. The relationship between the lack of appreciation for nature and a strong preference for technology is quite strong and observable. The relationship between education and nature is almost as pronounce as the former, as technological gadgets make people lazy with their study habits, causing them to resort to devices for tasks that historically had been done with the mind.

When people in a society judge their self-worth according to technological progress, it is materialistic. Materialism does not nourish the soul. Moreover, a materialistic soci ety will have a pattern of declining interests in the arts, culture, history, and in those fields that make a society spiritually rich. Material things cause people to forget about what is important. Also, products are distractions and addicting. All sources of addictions reduce self-control, defining the addicted person as a slave.

Moreover, a society composed of individuals obsessed with technological products will reject the protection of nature. Since most manufactured goods require natural resources for their production, all societies must negotiate the amount of goods they wish to produce with the available resources afforded by the environment. A society with a strong commitment to technological progress will therefore sacrifice the environment in order to manufacture the source that fuels their commitment, technology. A compromise cannot be met when the only option translates to death for the other party.

A society highly dependent on technology dulls their capacity for education. Since there are many products that aid in education, many students are dependent on mechanical devices. One such example is the calculator. In the past, students in math completed mathematical calculation with their agile minds. Nowadays, however, students are incap able of what had been considered in the past as simple computation, requiring devices to function in math courses. Human brains have not become less able mathematically since the last generation. The difference today is that technology has changed the study habits and expectations of students.

## Model Sentences of Essay # 58

1. A strong commitment for technological progress in a society tips the scale of social priorities by causing fundamental values such as education and environmentalism to be neglected.

2. Rampant materialism in a society does not appreciate the stimulus to the human soul that which is provided by non-material things.

3. A plastic product does not nourish the belief in sustaining nature, but instead it further destroys the forests, woods, mineral deposits and other environmental sources that help produce these technological products.

4. The relationship between education and nature is almost as pronounce as the former, as technological gadgets make people lazy with their study habits, causing them to resort to devices for tasks that historically had been done with the mind.

5. Moreover, a materialistic society will have a pattern of declining interests in the arts, culture, history, and in those fields that make a society spiritually rich.

6. Since most manufactured goods require natural resources for their production, all societies must negotiate the amount of goods they wish to produce with the available resources afforded by the environment.

7. A society with a strong commitment to technological progress will therefore sacrifice the environment in order to manufacture the source that fuels their commitment, technology.

8. A society highly dependent on technology dulls their capacity for education.

9. Nowadays, however, students are incapable of what had been considered in the past as simple computation, requiring devices to function in math courses.

10. The difference today is that technology has changed the study habits and expectations of students.

> 59. Should the government take responsibility for making sure that people lead healthy lives?

The government should not be entirely responsible for making sure that people lead healthy lives. The notion of free will should take precedence over matters that involve the personal choices of citizens. The right to choose a diet and lifestyle are up to the citizen and not the government. However, although the government should not interfere directly with personal choice, the government is entitled to nudge citizens on the right direction. Governments are within their rights to increase funding for education programs on healthy nutrition, and promote exercise and public parks.

There is a fine line between unacceptable government interference and practical public action. For example, the government of Denmark has enacted a Value Added Tax (VAT) on certain foods with high saturated fat, sugar or salt content. But citizens should have rights to consume these foods without government interference. Moreover many in the population are physically fit and healthy. The enactment of laws that target unhealthy foods is unfair, as it lumps together healthy and law-abiding citizens with citizens who are obese and unhealthy. Denmark is a country where the majority population, who are healthy, are penalized due to the actions and physical condition of the minority population. Such laws disenfranchising the majority population go against the values of representative democracies.

Governments are within their rights to point their finger to the direction that encourages healthy eating, allowing people to be educated on the facts and then having confidence in them to change their eating habits. The government could pour money into life management courses in their primary, and secondary schooling system. Steadily, with successive school years, young students eventually will mature into well-rounded eaters, having diets mirroring the requirements set by the Food and Drug Administration. The state and federal government are also within their right to mandate school districts to improve their cafeteria food. Measures such as these are practical policy measures that a government operating under a representative democracy is within their rights to follow.

Governments may also increase funding for the promotion of fitness parks. Since not every citizen is financially able to afford a gym membership, it is practical for governments to renovate and expand the numbers of their parks. Many parks have within their boundaries exercise areas tha t can withstand erosion from inclement weather. Such parks require minimum up keeping, saving the government from hiring expensive maintenance personnel.

In conclusion, there are many avenues governments can take to improve the health and wellbeing of citizens without being intrusive and abusive citizens' rights. It is not justifiable for governments to enact taxes discouraging the consumption of certain foods. Instead the proper course of action the government should take is to put into force practical measures which nudge the citizen on the right direction of healthy eating.

## Model Sentences of Essay # 59

1. The notion of free will should take precedence over matters that involve the personal choices of citizens.

2. However, although the government should not interfere directly with personal choice, the government is entitled to nudge citizens on the right direction.

3. There is a fine line between unacceptable government interference and practical public action.

4. The enactment of laws that target unhealthy foods is unfair, as it lumps together healthy and law-abiding citizens with citizens who are obese and unhealthy.

5. Denmark is a country where the majority population, who are healthy, are penalized due to the actions and

physical condition of the minority population.

6. Governments are within their rights to point their finger to the direction that encourages healthy eating, allowing people to be educated on the facts and then having confidence in them to change their eating habits.

7. Steadily, with successive school years, young students eventually will mature into well-rounded eaters, having diets mirroring the requirements set by the Food and Drug Administration.

8. Measures such as these are practical policy measures that a government operating under a representative democracy is within their right to follow.

9. Many parks have within their boundaries exercise areas that can withstand erosion from inclement weather.

10. Instead the proper course of action the government should take is to put into force practical measures that nudge the citizen in the right direction of healthy eating.

> 60. Should people adopt new ideas or values instead of relying on tradition?

People should not ignore the past and time honored traditions for sake of embracing new things, ideas, or values solely because they are novel inventions. There is value in a thing from the past that works, and positive significance to a tradition or belief that withstood the erosion of time. Sometimes traditions created by previous generations are useful and practical approaches to dealing with a social problem. According to Edmund Burke and his assessment of the French Revolution, old traditions came about from a complex process of negotiation between factors and successive generations that should not be blindly destroyed by younger generations merely because an idea is novel and full of idealism. New things, values, and ideas should be scrutinized in the same intensity as the traditions and values that are being challenged.

When the French Revolution of 1789 began its decade long march into anarchy and chaos, the supporters of the revolution were steeped in idealism and eager to wipe clean the society from old traditions. As a result, the pro-revolutionary government was ineffective. The size of French provinces were divided into equal sizes, as the revolutionary government preferred rationality in an idealized world over a realistic one, creating animosity in regions far from the capital city of Paris because ancient populations with ancient cultural ties were systematically made to be separate to conform with a cake cut in equal parts. The government made additional mistakes by confiscating church property. In the 1790s Revolutionary France had essentially adopted new ideas and destroyed centuries long traditions.

The British philosopher, Edmund Burke, published *Reflections on the Revolution in France* as a rebuke to the idealism of the French Revolution. He feared that Great Britain might succumb to the tide of revolutionary fervor from across the channel, as the temptation to destroy useful traditions for newer ideas became popular. Burke was proven correct in believing that the French Revolution would end disastrously because abstract notions, in the case with the revolutionary ideas of post-ancient France, ignore the complexities of human nature and society. With the case of France in the late 18th century, Burke believed that old ideas and traditions in government and society were being destroyed by unproven abstract ideas on liberty.

Despite the disastrous effects produced from policies passed by the pro-revolutionary government in France, there are instances in which new ideas and things should replace prior forms of behavior and things. Younger generations are able to evaluate the traditions of their parents and grandparents and make informed decisions. For example, the generation of 1960s America, their new values and liberal ideas on race and integration, gave rise to the eventual success of the Civil Rights movement. Giving political and economic rights to Black Americans were ideas that challenged old established traditions and ideas on race relations. Unlike the chaos of Revolutionary France, there are instances in which people should embrace novel ideas to improve the political and social situation of the times.

In conclusion, new things, values, and ideas should be scrutinized in the same intensity as the traditions and values that are being challenged. There is not enough reason to erase old traditions merely because they are old. In the same light, new ideas and values should not be adopted merely because they are new. As what Burke believed in relation to revolution in France, old traditions and values are created due to a complex process that should not be blindly destroyed by younger generations merely because an idea is novel and full of idealism.

## Model Sentences of Essay # 60

1. People should not ignore the past and time honored traditions for sake of embracing new things, ideas, or values solely because they are novel inventions.

2. Sometimes traditions created by previous generations are useful and practical approaches to dealing with a social problem.

3. According to Edmund Burke and his assessment of the French Revolution, old traditions came about from a complex process of negotiation between factors and successive generations that should not be blindly destroyed by younger generations merely because an idea is novel and full of idealism.

4. New things, values, and ideas should be scrutinized in the same intensity as the traditions and values that are being challenged.

5. When the French Revolution of 1789 began its decade long march into anarchy and chaos, the supporters of the

revolution were steeped in idealism and eager to wipe clean the society from old traditions.

6. He feared that Great Britain might succumb to the tide of revolutionary fervor from across the channel, as the temptation to destroy useful traditions for newer ideas became popular.

7. With the case of France in the late 18$^{th}$ century, Burke believed that old ideas and traditions in government and society were being destroyed by unproven abstract ideas on liberty.

7. Despite the disastrous effects produced from policies passed by the pro-revolutionary government in France, there are instances in which new ideas and things should replace prior forms of behavior and things.

8. For example, the generation of 1960s America, their new values and liberal ideas on race and integration, gave rise to the eventual success of the Civil Rights movement.

9. The size of French provinces were divided into equal sizes, as the revolutionary government preferred rationality in an idealized world over a realistic one, creating animosity in regions far from the capital city of Paris because ancient populations with ancient cultural ties were systematically made to be separate to conform with a cake cut in equal parts.

Printed in Great Britain
by Amazon